C000232942

liaison

liaison

liaison

William F. DeVault

liaison

©2021 Venetian Spider Press™
All rights reserved.
ISBN: 1-7349469-4-9
ISBN-13: 978-1-7349469-4-9

To Padua

Contents

Foreword

Main Street Books in Mansfield, Ohio was a quaint and energetic place with an upper balcony where guest readers could share poetry with the public. I was booked to read there on Saturday, October 19th, 2019. Preceding me was a rumor that William F. DeVault would be there for my reading. I knew of him and of his stellar reputation as a publisher, editor, and writer. My nerves shot skyward to think that I would finally meet the William F. DeVault. Moreover, I cringed to think that he would sit in judgment of my reading. When he arrived, he introduced himself to me and then took a seat at the back of the room. An hour later, he lauded my performance and invited me and his acquaintances to have lunch across the street. He and eleven others ambled to the restaurant where we basked in his intellectual repartee and keen wit. Evidence of his generosity surfaced when he offered to pay the entire bill for all of us. I sat across from him that day, practically spellbound by his vast reservoir of knowledge and his dead-on delivery of it. His mind demonstrated a cognitive reach beyond any person I'd ever met, and so I was not surprised when I read *liaison* and deemed it a triumph of content and structure.

Liaison is an heroic crown of heroic crowns of sonnets executed with such skill and craft that I fell into the rhythm immediately and wanted to read the entire work at one sitting. This is a collection that, from the first word to the last, moved me toward a recognition of perfection. It is an amazement of content, a manifestation of brilliance, and a masterwork of structure. Internal and end rhymes are rich and original with end rhymes enjambed perfectly. It is impossible to read a passage of any length from any of the fifteen heroic crowns without hearing the reverberations of assonance, consonants, and alliteration combining to make outstanding music on the page.

Content in *liaison* sweeps through the spectrum from autobiographical to erotic with spiritual and romantic stopping off points along the way. *Liaison* is "... as real as anything I have ever/ been witnessed to, true religion, ideal, / passionate in the extreme... " This author is "the gullible romantic" who would "... open my doors and welcome / you to my corner of the world... " A world in which the sum of everything is cause for celebration. The author does, indeed, make "... sense of the senselessness of the human heart."

Fresh imagery abounds throughout the poem and sex is beautifully expressed: "...wet slap / of body against body, frantic trance, / the animal soul we are born to trap / against the bed frame, a rhythmic dance." What about religion? It is "... rediscovered in delight." but " ... God does not bend to our muttering... " *Liaison* is passionate, raw, tender, and no word is wasted. Much of the word combinations are magnificent, and much of the poems are quotable. In the words of the author "...this book is like no other among my 25 plus volumes. It is what I have been training for more than half a century to produce. It is philosophical, autobiographical, spiritual, romantic, and erotic. It is me and my view of it all." This is a book "...tempered with love and life, joys and sorrows." This is a book I put forward as a masterpiece of writing.

R. Nikolas Macioci, Ph.D.
Author of *Why Dance?* and *Dark Guitar*
Columbus, Ohio, 2021

A very brief introduction

Poetry is violent act of self-revelation.

To me it is a focusing crystal that brooks no lies and reveals all if you look deep enough into it.

That I have birthed *liaison* in such a short period of time (written in 31 days) merely reinforces the necessity of the drowning man metaphor in my creativity. I drove myself to madness and exhaustion to best speak the truth, remembering specific people, incidents, and emotions, the better to speak of them in candor.

I owed and owe them that much.

My thanks to those who assisted in pulling this together and who stayed out of my way as I flung myself repeatedly off of cliffs of challenge and despair. I am content with this book, which is rare of me to say of my writing.

William F. DeVault

August 16, 2021

Pantheon

I Ghost of a chance, half dead but bled enough

Ghost of a chance, half dead but bled enough
to demonstrate the fluids of a youth
spilled, kissed with acolyte's reverence, tough
to measure, easy to treasure, the proof
of warm wine is in the pleasure released
in shadowed hallways and afternoon shade
that scarce reveals the luminescent beast
stalking our daydreams, walking in parade
under Brian's impassive gaze, union
that binds and breaks as we dare to partake
of a sullen and joyful communion
to sanctify our innocence and wake
all sleeping saints, our sanctification
to feed altars of the alteration.

II To feed altars of the alteration

To feed altars of the alteration,
we shed sackcloth and ash, flash and damper
to dive deep and sleep no more, frustration
itself frustrated, mated impure
and yet to an holy consecration
as this we do in remembrance of life
promised in two dimensional fictions
that told us more in sweaty afterlife
giggled about like naughty schoolchildren
with a secret that they think they alone
know about while the angels gossip then
bless us anyway, every star and stone
our secret, my feelings for you will bluff
the Goddesses and, yes, the lesser stuff.

III The Goddesses and, yes, the lesser stuff

The Goddesses and, yes, the lesser stuff
such as angels and imps, limp marathons
that race us to the horizons, your rough
breathing all the inspiration I need, yawns
as far away from this moment than thought
of more rational things, the eclectic
that lights the skies and your thighs caught and taut
like a spider's web, the cataleptic
dreams immolated into the actions
of a lover, birthing words for later
the amniotic fluids of passion's factions,
immortal and adamantine traitor,
our true natures, natural prophecy
of fifth material, obligation.

IIII Of fifth material, obligation

Of fifth material, obligation
to be true to the blue burned galactic
where was born the trace elements in sun
after sun after sun until the trick
became inevitable, our wise lies
bubbling over in a witches bright brew
fictional friction and diction of cries
that echo in hearts and souls to renew
the trouvere's truths to new generations
of lovers that are even now on path
to orbit until the obit says run
that was more of a meander, the math
reduced to simplest terms, others retreat
to a blue world without real fire to heat.

V To a blue world without real fire to heat

To a blue world without real fire to heat
cowards retreat, but I might die tonight
and am spiraling towards the center, sweet,
where you lay with me in cautious delight,
flowers and powers are for this magic
and we are immortal for a moment
or two as we celebrate the tragic
truth that there are coins to be spent and sent
in messages to future and present -
denials of yesterdays that grow pale
as we tell the stories behind recent
reckonings, as we cannot bear the grail
forever, we drink deeply great, sweet kegs,
sweet lips and slender hips that beg the dregs.

VI Sweet lips and slender hips that beg the dregs

Sweet lips and slender hips that beg the dregs
find in me an enthusiasm, high
on your beauty and the barter and beg
of one more moment, one more hour, to try
as we might to hold back the universe
with our hunger and desires, the fires blaze
to our own immolations, blinding God
and all angels to an ascendent gaze
that finds a flicker of unity that
would dare survive strange and notorious
in the flesh, but immortal in word, spat,
whispered by swain with intent glorious
to love gods forgot, a part formed conceit
to be transfigured into more complete.

VII To be transfigured into more complete

To be transfigured into more complete
dreamers, we must dream as we lay, awake
to take sustenance in our savage sweet
surrenders and victories, hills we take
and valleys we taste in explorations
of conquered territories, advising
mercy and restraint as we paint stations
of our own cross and in sacred rising
from tombs of our blasphemic mutterings,
forgiven for our enthusiasms,
trespass of skin and sin and offerings
given in sacrifices in spasms
that burn these moments, ritual that begs
idolatry, balsa to stone, long legs.

VIII Idolatry, balsa to stone, long legs

Idolatry, balsa to stone, long legs,
tentacles of an elegant kraken
dragging me down to a beauty that begs
all previous understandings, a zen
of tender passions that belies the words
of all I had ever read, bland bread fed
in crumbs as if to hungry beasts and birds
to placate but not nourish with truths said
only in the least honest and ornate
manner possible. The Poitiers Court
made sport of by shy minstrels who would fate
us all to shades of grey, you know the sort,
those who would belie and deny the dance
on which stands generations of romance,

VIIII On which stands generations of romance

On which stands generations of romance,
the monuments of this moment, the thought
that somehow the divine is wine to chance
on perfect sip while in cold cages caught
by the façade, the charade, this life's shade,
made for us in an approximation
of what we were led to expect, cascade
and serenade of the peddlers fiction
we buy as we are used to a nothing
that strips away the beauty of your smile
every bit as nervous as mine, we bring
our earnest doubts and will share for a while
our true desire, anticipating dawn
the dance of decades yet uncertain, gone.

X The dance of decades yet uncertain, gone

The dance of decades yet uncertain, gone
is transient doubt that we may not find
the missing pieces to the puzzles on
which we would stake our souls and bind our blind
visions of beauty in the universe
where flowers wither and die and we cry,
cry like lost children in the cold, cold curse
of the isolation and as we scry
the other side, another side still fades
and our hearts are damned to turn to a grey
like tasteless communion wafers and blades
carve bloodless flesh for the whims and the worms
in the instant silence alone, by chance,
before we contemplate in mystic's trance.

XI Before we contemplate in mystic's trance

Before we contemplate in mystic's trance
the nature of our pleasure, our treasure
discovered, uncovered, recovered, chance
playing fair with us for once, I measure
the distance from the edge of sanity
I have travelled in mere moments, confess
false idols I have taken, vanity
commanding and corrupting into less
than the worthiest of the heart's wishes,
saved from twisted thoughts and mislaid daydreams
that set upon me and sought militias
of demons and dark thoughts to best the themes
of passion and prayers before I was gone -
the oracle's perfect kiss set upon.

XII The oracle's perfect kiss set upon

The oracle's perfect kiss set upon
young lovers, healing the terrible scars
we buried, we carried, malign and spawn
of festering sorrows, the proto stars
we must transcend to be more than debris
on the bleak battlefields of awareness
where virtue is a bangle bought in three
fragments to decorate our nakedness.
Too far afield we wandered before now
and now is when and where and how we find
that we are not simple machines that bow
to the brutality of fate, unkind
not as we have been bent, it is our right,
us to feast in red and white through the night

XIII Us, to feast in red and white through the night

Us, to feast in red and white through the night.
Us, to find fit fittings to our desires,
fires finding better fall than down, our sight
returning in what unity requires.
We are no longer twain lost, tragic souls
but merged halves of a genesis fusion,
our nature is not rude solitude, coals
burning in our skulls seek an inclusion
in joy and peace, the release of sorrows
as tomorrow seeks to break us, make us
just another chalk outline in furrows
left by the Jagannath cart to take us
down and leave little remains, so we fight,
religion rediscovered in delight.

XIIII Religion rediscovered in delight

Religion rediscovered in delight.
you are perfect image of my rapture.
You are my Goddess, I am acolyte,
and I will go where you will and capture
stars in jars and be at peace with our time
we share when we care or dare to make prayers
with our bodies and our hearts, reason, rhyme,
and the persistence of your voice that dares
to call you mine without hesitation
when I would assent and without relent
in deepest meander of fate, I shun
all that I was and wished, will not repent
for the turn of the dice, daring rebuff,
ghost of a chance, half dead but bled enough.

XV Ghost of a chance, half dead but bled enough (diadem)

Ghost of a chance, half dead but bled enough
to feed altars of the alteration.
The Goddesses and, yes, the lesser stuff
of fifth material, obligation
to a blue world without real fire to heat
sweet lips and slender hips that beg the dregs
to be transfigured into more complete
idolatry, balsa to stone, long legs
on which stands generations of romance,
the dance of decades yet uncertain, gone
before we contemplate in mystic's trance
the oracle's perfect kiss set upon
us to feast in red and white through the night
religion rediscovered in delight.

Rapprochement

I Peace be with you, even if hard won, sin?

Peace be with you, even if hard won, sin?
War with ourselves, battle often foolish
when built on the thinnest of pretense, kin
to self-mutilation, path to ghoulish
necromantic dances with our nightmares,
for fear is the great disabler, it steals
all real context and content of affairs
of the heart and the upstart love that seals
bright moments from the darkest days and nights,
giving us retribution for our pain,
doubts, damages inevitable, lights
obscured by our own blinding cut and stain
we touch in hopeful communications,
intimacy, and negotiations.

II intimacy and negotiations

intimacy and negotiations
brokered when your hands seek to study me
as map of the pleasures the creations
of kisses and your clever tongue to see
what sibilant sighs you may evidence
as my surrender to your empathy
and seeming infinite soft elements
haunting, taunting me to rise so you see
how much my desire transcends sanity
and every opening to make peace
and love and surrender the white wine, free
of hesitation on command, release
delayed just by your flesh's rebellion
wound around the wounds and tenderest sin.

III Wound around the wounds and tenderest sin

Wound around the wounds and tenderest sin,
the latex phylactery barely sheathes
as the point is taken and given in
martyrdom to a purpose to yet seethe
with the exquisite power of capture,
the power you have over me expressed
long before we undressed, sustained rapture
in the sheen of sweat and desires confessed
in guttural whispers and the wet slap
of body against body, frantic trance,
the animal soul we are born to trap
against the bedframe, in a rhythmic dance
of finding common grinding, foundations
we surrender to remember, stations!

IIII we surrender to remember, stations

we surrender to remember, stations
of a cross upon which you would be hung
if you could, crucifixion fixation,
your sacrifice for the songs to be sung
in wordless rhapsody, a melody
that rages in stages of excitement,
reaching crescendo several times, free
verse and rhythmic, atonal incitement,
I want to hear your song for it inspires
me to greater joy, releasing lions
and my loins to fulfill oaths and the fires
to light skies and your eyes with the ions
of irony, pleasure and pain, a kiss
on the road to happiness and the bliss.

V On the road to happiness and the bliss

On the road to happiness and the bliss,
I trace ripe rivulets across your flesh
as I tease the pink meringues with a kiss
that lingers in the sweetness, and the fresh
heat of your arousal, heaven and earth,
birthed in the better angels of our merge,
urgent rhythms that sustain us, we birth
new legend in your crucible and scourge
ourselves to raw tissues that taste of haste
as we feast in gluttonous joy, transport
and the flickering ticket as we raced
our pulses and pulsed our releases, sport
and liturgy, frantic tantric commenced,
the trajectory of language, silenced.

VI The trajectory of language, silenced

The trajectory of language, silenced
by the sounds of lovemaking, forgiveness
for past and present trespasses, pretensed
in the tension of lovers' eagerness
to live the instant, the nanosecond
where heartbeats share the line of sound, of sight,
and no you or I, unity beckoned
and we were willing traitors to the night
mocking the stalking horses of belief
that this is more than simple liaison:
Even barren, we are Eden and reef
to a million new lives, phenomenon
romanticized to tell what critics miss
in gentle touch and a tentative kiss.

VII in gentle touch and a tentative kiss

in gentle touch and a tentative kiss
we communicate our needs and our prayers,
making a religion of a new bliss,
our carnal communion on chapel stairs
sacrilege and a passionate coeur rage
that knows no quench or quiet, unashamed
of the degrees at which we burn, the stage
set and wet within a moment's thought framed
by the visions we have summoned and find
fit fuel for the cooling immolation
that burns us into sanity, and blind
Polyphemus foresaw consummation,
in our true natures, no defense against
seeking assurance, endurance licensed.

VIII seeking assurance, endurance licensed

seeking assurance, endurance licensed
by the very nature of our pure states,
impure of thought but caught in war against
the limits jealous, zealous rule dictates
as they try to strip us of our needs,
naked for the touch and taste of our bodies,
plundering wonder for the passion seeds
that were not the downfall of the species…
if was disobedience, defiance,
and the desire to know as God would know,
not to find the matching parts' alliance
for hearts to express in a perfect flow
of boundaries torn and reborn to surge
in the entwined fingers and legs that merge.

VIIII in the entwined fingers and legs that merge

in the entwined fingers and legs that merge
as we reach the ignition point of all,
melting our madness to find a new purge
as we emerge into a quickened fall
softly to our euphoric underworld
where we rule in giggled revelations
and we are given to give and live, curled
into the center of a creation
where miracles heal and seal contusions
of our doubts and harsh words the old, cold world
had learned to live with, bitter philters run
from the veins of the befouled who have furled
the secret scrolls and runes set to destroy
our essences in a remembranced joy.

X Our essences in a remembranced joy!

Our essences in a remembranced joy!
To be as children, still discovering
that life is colors and flavors, alloy
of all the substances imagining
can bring to us to dance like tongues in soft
communications, held as important
tactile semaphore to beg an aloft
sensibility to this sacred cant
as we take turns taking our feed, to bleed
emotions at a tantalus pace, face
to face with your beauty, fulfill my need,
find a manner of contact that can trace
my scars on the mandylion in surge
that explodes like the fireworks that can purge.

XI That explodes like the fireworks that can purge

That explodes like the fireworks that can purge
this world of the greyest fragments, sorrow
satiated to burn like black powder, verge
on the Planck fever then push tomorrow
further down the road, goad of flesh and pricked
by your beauty and attentions, for you
and none other, the channel warm and slicked
with expectations of receiving true
the sacrament shared only by earnest
and enthusiastic acolytes, heat
and the ancient brain conspiring to wrest
all the mediocrities and defeat,
the stale devils of our profoundest doubts
the bitter moments that bid to destroy.

XII The bitter moments that bid to destroy

The bitter moments that bid to destroy,
to twist and resist all things of beauty,
the road to entropy we deny, joy
and delight, the light in the night, duty
of the lovers to hold back the night, bright
with hope and elation, we mount our war
in hours of drills and skills to practice right
manners of incursion into our souls
bitter taste of fear lost to a tear wept
in sudden awareness, a cry of dreams
becoming a mark for the castle kept
and repeatedly won anew, true themes
of our bold heroic revelation
the essence of our illumination.

XIII The essence of our illumination

The essence of our illumination.
Our magnitude of rude remembrances
sparking still the fire of revolution
as we have found our own chase and chances
the elegy is not yet written, I
am baptized and consecrated by sweat
that between us is waters holy, scry
to this prophecy. I am burning wet
to your holy waters as I take yet
a deeper draught to your profound delight,
I am smitten by a hermit's trance to whet
and wet my lips every way tonight
holding purpose against those whose station:
To banish light from life from salvation.

XIIII To banish light from life from salvation

To banish light from life from salvation
seems to be the most perfidious goal
of more than one huckster preacher, ration
of bitter herbs has stolen their joy, toll
of cracked bells and dry-tongued choirs, liars
of a ravening mediocrity
seeking to trample us underfoot, briars
to make into crowns of a self-pity
that would damn us with their judgement, bitter
as the dregs of poisoned wine, divine lies
that seek to strip our nakedness, split her
and I into haploid sorrows for prize
given by themselves within their hate, thin
peace be with you, even if hard won sin.

XV Peace be with you, even if hard won, sin (diadem)

Peace be with you, even if hard won, sin,
intimacy, and negotiations
wound around the wounds and tenderest win
we surrender to remember, stations
on the road to happiness and the bliss,
the trajectory of language, silenced
in gentle touch and a tentative kiss
seeking assurance, endurance licensed
in the entwined fingers and legs that merge
our essences in a remembranced joy
that explodes like the fireworks that can purge
the bitter moments that bid to destroy
the essence of our illumination
to banish light from life from salvation.

Amazon

I The measure of epic legerdemain

The measure of epic legerdemain.
Mesmeric and the heretic just smiles
at the thought of ascending the domain
of the senses until, hours and miles
behind us, we are insensate, content
and wondering where the time and world went
when we were focused on thoughts more urgent
(if thought was what you could call firmament
falling away in glissando sighs and
prehensile touch of tongue and fingertips
when the sheets no longer provide, for hand,
opportunity to hold on as slips
the vines of war and love and your flytrap
from toe to hip to let slip and to wrap.)

II from toe to hip to let slip and to wrap

from toe to hip to let slip and to wrap,
your legs cage me as you promised they would,
warm and muscular, lean and to bootstrap
conversations of an unspoken good,
playing guardrails to guide me to the rhythm
of your hunger, ankles locked and loaded
to goad me to reward, algorithm,
equation with barriers eroded
until nothing is holding us back in
doubt or desperation, consummation
a consecration, Holy water, sin,
silently speaking in tongues, to ration
lovers' sacrament, Mandylion's stain.
twin serpents to guard your Eden, champagne.

III twin serpents to guard your Eden, champagne

twin serpents to guard your Eden, champagne
with the taste of honeysuckle, jasmine,
warm at issuance, relinquishing pain
to stain only my dreams, spasm, chasm
and the bridge that a thousand burnings failed
to keep us apart, the start and the end,
morning vespers then evening walls scaled
to lay with you in the private garden
running my hands through your hair as you tear
my fabric and flesh to encourage life
to perform as it should, with fierce and fair
devotion, sorrows lost, conquering strife
for we are drunk on the wine of this trap
to uncork, and to coit and calm and slap.

IIII To uncork, and to coit and calm and slap

To uncork, and to coit and calm and slap,
away or to spur more the racehorse rhythms
drive until the purpose blurs and spurs wrap
our pain in the revelation of love
and pleasure and the ecstasy of dreams
that diminish Elysium, above
all other purpose in this moment, screams
that echo through the trees and in the breeze
of ten thousand generations now gone
and yet to come and find fault when we seize
the moment and turn ourselves to the dawn
to crumble to dust but the refreshing,
flesh to flesh, in the threshing of meshing.

V flesh to flesh, in the threshing of meshing

flesh to flesh, in the threshing of meshing.
the grain goes against us, we are reborn
in the image of the gods, confessing
that we are woven of gossamer, scorn
us for our delight in the night of dance
in the majesty of your thighs, where once
I found my foolscap, but am now by chance
and your persistence, no longer the dunce
ardently reciting catechism
against the pillows and between your legs
as you flutter on rapture's edge, prism
to light fantastic with colour that begs
a new definition of a vision
to mark a common path, fleeting heaven.

VI to mark a common path, fleeting heaven

to mark a common path, fleeting heaven
still not beyond our grasp or gasp, invoke
the most essential essence of passion
and demand your sustenance as you yoke
me to your fit fantasies and straddle
me to take a ride to the land of dreams
my hair as bridle, you spur me, saddle
for this carnal canter that answers themes
of merger of awe and affection, kissed
with cunning encouragement to summon
the mountaintop mantras so often missed.
reassurances run white and red in
sweat slicked fine fuckery and the meshing,
to rebound and return, a refreshing.

VII to rebound and return, a refreshing

to rebound and return, a refreshing
of our souls and satiations, burning
us alive and to life as we are threshing
out of the chaff the kernels of yearning
popped and properly improper to stop
the ennui of hot afternoons we spent
exploring with probing prayers to sop
the bread and drink the wine of sacrament
made mortal divinity, transient, moist
as the soul kiss of missing meanders
demanding a path to where we had voiced
our purposes and passions as strangers
to the promises we made to heaven
of the silent oaths we spoke to deafen.

VIII of the silent oaths we spoke to deafen

of the silent oaths we spoke to deafen
voyeuristic angels who did not judge
but showed earnest concern that we deaden
more than the pain and stain and greedy grudge
against those who held us back before we
found key and lock and made an alliance
against the grey agents of gravity
that would steal our wings and forbid this dance
in which we find light and touch and glory
of a magnitude undenied by those
who understand the grandness of story
writ in tongues and fingertips on shed clothes
as sigil and ward as we burned to blue
our hesitations, as I carried you.

VIIII our hesitations, as I carried you

our hesitations, as I carried you
as a pantomime of the wedding won
in patience and a testament so true
that you carved it in my memory, done
is doubt, done is holding back the cascade
of word and thought and touch and taste and eyes
that bear witness in joy and wonder played
against silhouette of perfected prize
resurrected time and again to split thighs
and rise as far as you care and dare take
my sacrifice and surrender, the cries
of pilgrims this communion to partake,
of acolytes of love, in words we spoke
through doorway to bed, arrogance awoke.

X through doorway to bed, arrogance awoke

through doorway to bed, arrogance awoke
along with the fireworks of fantasies
liberating tantalus ardor, broke
like water over a great dam, we please
ourselves and one another, congruent
caterwauls and the fall of ancient stone
as I find your golden calves and thighs, bent
to my worship and liturgy, alone
to our understanding as we now speak
in tongues and transient flashes and flushes
that rise like a new found pink sun to leak
sudden awareness, this light banishes
shadows of old apocalypse we hew
by the assent you gave in word, and new.

XI by the assent you gave in word and new

by the assent you gave in word and new
to my universe, we find singular
form to warm our cold extremities, blue
with chill emitted by this low set bar
that slaps us down for mediocrity,
demanding we grovel in the gravel
for less than nothing, the fates' enmity
expressed in bitter disappointment spell

of underachieving prophets, who lose
their validity in the great nothings
promised without delivery, they choose
to miss the point we find in yet some things
you summon with a whisper, a white smoke
surrender, conquest of me when you spoke.

XII surrender, conquest of me when you spoke

surrender, conquest of me when you spoke
words of rudest seduction, engaging
my heart and other parts in the time woke
to the brilliance of your exuberance
and your bashful ambivalence doubting
that your confection would be missed by me
as it had been missed by you in shouting
silence and the violence of fear, free
from the truth that you are perfect and I,
I am but suitor to Persephone
with nothing to offer that you may buy
with your laugh and smile and all that I see
that reverberates in poet's peruse,
words of love and desire, skyscraper muse.

XIII words of love and desire, skyscraper muse

words of love and desire, skyscraper muse,
my offer to you. all else, time and dust,
I am offering to you, if you choose,
immortality that does not fade, rust,
or remain in the ephemeral, pale
and dying, I grant this for your favor,
for that is the true power of this grail
that I carry and choose to share, savour
and scent, to see future generations
and even those beyond, surrender heart
to your grace and face and place in stations
of dreams, forever, the essential part
to the clockwork hearts, my angel and muse.
I kiss your beauty, and never refuse.

XIIII I kiss your beauty, and never refuse

I kiss your beauty, and never refuse
to be with you, banking fires that must wait
until later. You are my angel, muse
and friend, illumination to the state
of the universe so I might finally
see with eyes in yet another spectrum,
finding mysteries and histories free
of the nature of life, to not succumb
to the temptation to fade into grey
without an appreciation of love
beyond self-love, finding my fumbling way
with hope born of our unity, above
the common cliches of pleasure and pain.
The measure of epic legerdemain.

The measure of epic legerdemain.
from toe to hip to let slip and to wrap,
twin serpents to guard your Eden, champagne
to uncork, and to coit and calm and slap
flesh to flesh, in the threshing of meshing
to mark a common path, fleeting heaven
to rebound and return, a refreshing
of the silent oaths we spoke to deafen
our hesitations, as I carried you
through doorway to bed, arrogance awoke
by the assent you gave in word and new
surrender, conquest of me when you spoke
words of love and desire, skyscraper muse,
I kiss your beauty, and never refuse.

Babylon

I the lights are brightest at night, we are not

the lights are brightest at night, we are not,
as our feral natures take us down, swift
with the grift that somehow love is lust, caught
in our webs of words and neon we drift
against the tide of our timidity
brash and only slightly aware of what
we are in pursuing morbidity
over our better natures, and when that
catches the karma boomerang we hang
our heads and wake up tomorrow to start
the whole process over again, harangue
for our aching head and broken bed, heart
against hopes, we mangle the minuet,
falling and fumbling, into desire wet.

II falling and fumbling, into desire wet

falling and fumbling, into desire wet
we dive, rampant against rampart plunder
of the thunder and the arched limbs we get
tangled up in, twins but not twain, under
the drab slab of heaven we now labor
looking for the slightest release to feast
until we are sated, but with saber
sheathed in satin sleeve for the most and least
of intemperances, dancing music
we make in our beds and heads and hopeful
that this time, this time, we share fluidic
forgetfulness, pass ourselves to cope, full
of that which we can share what we have got
with the amniotics of ideas, hot.

III with the amniotics of ideas, hot

with the amniotics of ideas, hot
we are, heated and depleted but still
driven by insatiable thirst, not
to be quenched as we rewrite with our quill
the record books, marvel our staminas
as we shake loose the earthquakes that pound us
that confound us with their merged animas,
forged formulae for sums that confound us
swept out in not so lazy afternoons
to relinquish our subtler tasks and asks
in deliverance of blessed new moons
where memory is shaded in fresh basks
under a sun of our radiance, whet
and focused on the hocus pocus jet

IIII And focused on the hocus pocus jet

And focused on the hocus pocus jet
every angle is tangled, hard and soft
we slide and glide and, inside, pirouette
to a fevered dance, a tango aloft
in the skies of our afterthoughts forgot
that gravity itself is suspended
to the sound of unbound ecstasy, not
more than less than all of the upended
bed and pillow and rug and hardwood floor
we swore we'd get to sooner or later
and now seems as good of a time to score
yet another bullseye for the greater
prone sharpshooters, hidden by fragrant vine
of jasmine and honeysuckle, warm wine.

V Of jasmine and honeysuckle, warm wine

Of jasmine and honeysuckle, warm wine
spills so many times that we have lost count
and it is irrelevant, more than fine
as I divine your new needs to my mount.
You kiss like an orchard of lost Eden,
intoxicating and celebrating
the true nature of life and the season
of our intemperate joy, creating
opportunities for insight, delight
and blinding brightness that in brisance flares
to obscure the solitudes of the night
where we find ancient moments for the scarce
monuments in hearts complementary,
spilt and split in the sedimentary.

VI spilt and split in the sedimentary

spilt and split in the sedimentary
stones and riverbanks of time, where goes time
around the distant turn, momentary
ecstasies extract their toll and the prime
of our youths wearies and weathers our skin
but not our synaptic memories, smiles
summoned with a thought, a scent that pulls in
the happiness I felt with you and miles
melt to the inches or less we caressed
one another from, hands like faith healers
spreading warmth and restoring our repressed
and seemingly forgotten time, dealers
from a Tarot deck of song of benign,
remnants of last night, another divine.

VII remnants of last night, another divine

remnants of last night, another divine
chapter in a secret volume larger
than the sacred scriptures that we consign
our immortal souls to set our merger
with an hostile universe, not evil
but like a night's blizzard, not conducive
to our survival without upheaval
in the natural order, abusive
de facto, but without malevolence
to set purpose and patterns. in covert
we write our own histories, evidence
in memories and scratches, the overt
to us, we make the past what we parry,
revealed to be failed perception, faerie.

VIII revealed to be failed perception, faerie

revealed to be failed perception, faerie,
the glamor of mediocrity, grey,
of a settlement upon things very
unworthy of our pain and passions, weigh
the value of our entanglement, bind
the greater good to a still greatest good.
we kiss like candidates for kinship, blind
to the edge of the world we know we should
avoid, but the fall is auspicious,
as are you, and your hunger burns as brand.
nothing is worse that disingenuous
touch and tumble, stumbling on to the grand
finale descending, fire lubricious
as something more malicious, delicious.

VIIII As something more malicious, delicious

As something more malicious, delicious.
and sweet, as I find when I take you pure,
lips and tongue and fingertips ambitious
in their explorations of your pleasure
measured in the rising sparks and shudder
I feel through you as you pass barriers
that stood between you and your swift judder
of expressed release, sought by harriers
of empathic tenderness, finding right
pathways to the fire once you kept hidden
but have blessed me with the vision, a sight
of where you would have me touch, trace again
the passage to the well of your conceit.
but ultimately unnourishing, sweet.

X But ultimately unnourishing, sweet

But ultimately unnourishing, sweet
as spun sugar, sustaining us not, but
grant reward for proprieties retreat
to allow us solemn gayeties, cut
from our most elusive fantasies, found
in our own truest, bluest needs and seeds
to grow as the passionate vine in ground
that you define as the vineyards, your greed
to share, to care, to dare. I am with you
on this journey to the furthest reaches
where we alone will lay together, true
to our hearts and undying on beaches
of white sand, if we doubt, made poisonous
and corrosive, the path is lost to us.

XI And corrosive, the path is lost to us

And corrosive, the path is lost to us
for we must find firm footings to keep up
above the deadly waters, bent to truss
with tides and snide nixies who fill their cup
with tears and fears such as we may possess,
flying high above the darkest abyss
to insinuate that yes, we confess
to our greater and lesser sins, to kiss
fate and hate and hope and petulant dawns
where we find ourselves too often in bleak
landscapes, scraped from mysteries of old bronze
overwhelmed by newer alloys, the peak
never achieved, yet we strive, we compete!
there is ample guilt, but the quest? defeat!

XII there is ample guilt, but the quest? defeat

there is ample guilt, but the quest? defeat
is the illumination of carnage
left in our wakes, the stakes? life or death beat
down to coins of contrition, prophets rage
the pages are turned as always, language
forming one means of communication
that corrupts so readily, the frail cage
in which we place our hearts for protection
will not withstand the perfidy of false
lovers, poisoning us with words not meant
as anything but night dancers who waltz
and glide in mockery as what was spent
is a poison in a mortuary
not a word in my vocabulary.

XIII not a word in my vocabulary

not a word in my vocabulary
is wasted, I have tasted tears, spat out
the trace venoms of false lovers, very
near to death have I breathed a fiery gout
to press back the angry hordes, their swords drawn
in fear and speculation of what I
demand of them when I appear and spawn
amomancies both bright and dark, no lie
in my pronouncements, but the earnest proof
that love is regent in all of its forms,
breaking bonds and hearts making urgent hoof
to the cobblestones before coming storms
obscure the fallen dragon and faerie
as I draw curtains to angels' aery.

XIIII as I draw curtains to angels' aery

as I draw curtains to angels' aery
I part them to your chambers where you wait
for a promised night of passions, very
different than the muddy mead of fate
that you have observed and tasted, wasted
on such as you, who should rule the midnight
and the sun, done with the nothings pasted
instead of carved, their limp dictions in spite
of their true natures already revealed
by their very ignorance of the craft
the most holy house of the poets wield
played against a flourish of mere stagecraft.
we hide in shadows to observe a thought:
the lights are brightest at night, we are not.

the lights are brightest at night, we are not,
falling and fumbling, into desire wet
with the amniotics of ideas, hot
and focused on the hocus pocus jet
of jasmine and honeysuckle, warm wine
spilt and split in the sedimentary
remnants of last night, another divine
revealed to be failed perception, faerie
as something more malicious, delicious
but ultimately unnourishing, sweet
and corrosive, the path is lost, to us
there is ample guilt, but the quest? defeat
not a word in my vocabulary
as I draw curtains to angels' aery.

lay hands on

I lay your hands on me, drawing out venom

lay your hands on me, drawing out venom
that steals our strength, seals our cold sepulcher
to languish in half-life greying to come
to entropies in a bleak sepulture
where we care so little for such few things
we are revenants and wisps of a life
abandoned by the side of the road, kings
and beggars forget we ever lived, knife
to and through the heart of our muttering,
prayers that fall not on deaf ears, but the will
of God does not bend to our murmuring,
we must make our case as the lovers still
undefeated, banishing attitude
of the surrender to bleak solitude.

II of the surrender to bleak solitude

of the surrender to bleak solitude
when the scent of your exotic lotion
breaks and shakes my reverie, welcome rude
intrusion into my mind, devotion
to a passionate goddess who whispers
sweet vulgarities to me, distracting
me from somber doubts to playful vespers
recited in delighted refracting
of grey into thousands of bright rainbows
that dance across your warm form as I chase
them like a cat in daydreams of hunt, rows
of dominoes toppled, my measured face
placed between thighs to banish gloom and glum
that poisons a soul and heart to benumb.

III that poisons a soul and heart to benumb

that poisons a soul and heart to benumb
is not to entertain or let remain
in the sunshine of the day or to plumb
the depths of our ardor and pleasured pain
as we rend barriers and open way
to the earnest hedonism of youth
where we study our spellcraft and we play
preparations, frantic fanatic truth

to let our fires rise and fall, infrared
to the blue-white magnetar that draws us
to the beckoning bed. When all is said
rutting animals, the fever claws us
and transforms us to feral and quite nude
the shattered nerves that serve an attitude.

IIII the shattered nerves that serve an attitude

the shattered nerves that serve an attitude
or an aspect of the moment's mission
is lost to us if we do not coil, lewd
semblances of dancers in transition
from strangers to fierce lovers, repenting
nothing but how long it took to capture
the fever and amplify it, burning
more than fingertips as it slips to cure
us of a doomsday melancholia
such that we laugh in the grace and the face
of self-immolation, the phobia
of losing oneself lost in a blind race
that debrides the dangerous serenade
of self-loathing as fit feast to the fade.

V of self-loathing as fit feast to the fade

of self-loathing as fit feast to the fade.
of pretense bent and flexed until perplexed
enough to lose all understanding, laid
tracks to the horizon, rails that once vexed
our illusions and set us on a slide
across satin sheets, acceleration
in frank frenzy to the fireflowers, ride
me until I feel nothing but you, stun
me with the power of cacophonic
invocations, call me to sacrifice
fluids and sentience to your sonic
tonic for my sadness, madness paid price
as we rise and run, again, rise and run,
from effervescence to the stagnation.

VI from effervescence to the stagnation

from effervescence to the stagnation
of fluids wasted or tasted in shy
surrender, wanton exuberance run
roughshod over paths tender that belie
how inadequate our hearts' thesaurus
is in giving us the words that alone
reveal the poetry, repenting puss
and cockerel the menagerie grown
to overwhelm our better senses, hot
with a fire like a forge gone blue and white
in a night of infernal sweetness shot
with the coals of our desire, burning bright
to illuminate our troubled charade
of loneliness, far from this serenade.

VII Of loneliness, far from this serenade

Of loneliness, far from this serenade,
of bitterness and regret, the flop sweat,
the endless walk, salty senseless parade
of desperation, stumbling, fumbling threat
of annihilation, degradation
and the remnants and revenants of prayers
that were not really to God, but homespun
idols and graven images, affairs
not of the heart, but plutonic organs,
screaming their mating calls in hot hormones
that ignore real hunger and thirst, gorgons
turning frail fleshes into tempered stones
the better to find your mind's translation,
words that make wishes, make excitation.

VIII words that make wishes, make excitation

words that make wishes, make excitation
the fantasy that what is really was
as we play permeable souls, passion
and affection focusing when we pause
to adjust to an inconstant platform
that is one another's bodies taking
turns at playing Atlas to the warm norm
now heated incendiary, breaking
to wet the sheets and whet our appetites
as delights beyond the Turkish barter
for a philanthropic tropic that lights
the darkness in all the senses, martyr
to your demand and command, fever fed
for your better use of me in the bed.

VIIII for your better use of me in the bed

for your better use of me in the bed
I have followed the practices that please
and have kissed the bright flower that has bled
soft fragrance for my enticement, at ease
with the truth: there is no higher worship
than to do what your deity desires
and light the fires before rending veils, rip
and slip and drip and when passion conspires
to transfigure two to one in courtly
ceremony and mysteries of true
love gods of forgotten religions, free
such that Poiters court itself would judge coup
of the five faiths and zealous wraiths, manic,
where we draw out the magic and music.

X where we draw out the magic and music

where we draw out the magic and music
we leave behind a spark divine, warm wine
comingled with the jasmine, the tantric
traps sprung and we take thick the fine combine,
consuming in the consummation, gasp
and exhalation of exultation
as the rites spite the pretense of our grasp
exceeding pale reaches, imitation
of Michelangelo on the ceiling,
feeling everything and singing the cant
of the lovers, bartering the sealing
of a promise made and manifest scant
moments ago, white candles by the bed
when we lay hands on one another, red.

XI when we lay hands on one another, red

when we lay hands on one another, red
are the warning lights that flash as we coit
and spark, solferino flint, my steel, bed
as magic carpet on which we exploit
our own sorcery, sweet and savory
and with a self-conceived gout of a fire
that catches us in the inferno, free
of guilt and second thoughts, sacred desire
besting better judgements as we see smoke
from our frictions, fictions notwithstanding
with coy words and tenderness that is spoke
in playful reverence in this branding,
souls hypergolic, burning brandies lick
lips to white wine to drafts therapeutic.

XII lips to white wine to drafts therapeutic

lips to white wine to drafts therapeutic
for our cracked and battered souls, the solace
in the arms of lovers when heretic
hearts declare a newer testament, face
to face, dancers draped in damask petals,
laughing with joy, the moment is regent,
our freedom is seemingly of metals
from another sphere, alloyed to prevent
the naysayers and players of false cards
opportunity to declare our fates
in the craven haven of bitter shards
piercing skin to drag us down to their gates
as we find beauty in the thirsts we slake
and sustained to release tensions we take.

XIII And sustained to release tensions we take

And sustained to release tensions we take
an overdose of blended pheromone,
your breasts beg my lips, as do your hips, snake
charmer and chalice of the holy throne
where has sat too many pretenders, frail
falsehoods born as much from our hungry dreams
as from their perfidies, we buy lies, grail
of the charlatans who live in the themes
of poets and philosophers shouting
pretty words to dubious hearts, jaded
faded usurpers, given to doubting
evident truths when inconvenient, dead
to the life rising in the heat we make
as fuel to our frenzies, the thirsts we slake.

XIIII as fuel to our frenzies, the thirsts we slake

as fuel to our frenzies, the thirsts we slake,
to your eternal, infernal pleasures
my tongue and lips between your hips, awake
to the sensations I spark as treasures
to be banked against your hungers, small deaths
that do not seem so small when your nerves fire
and you are gripping the sheets, our hot breaths
making circuit of the eclectic wire
that runs between and through us as you arch
your back and speak in languages unknown
since the fall of Eden, where we demarche
our negotiated release, seeds sown
to bloom in impossible flowers, come,
lay your hands on me, drawing out venom.

lay your hands on me, drawing out venom
of the surrender to bleak solitude
that poisons a soul and heart to benumb
the shattered nerves that serve an attitude
of self-loathing as fit feast to the fade
from effervescence to the stagnation
of loneliness, far from this serenade
words that make wishes make excitation
for your better use of me in the bed
where we draw out the magic and music
when we lay hands on one another, red
lips to white wine to drafts therapeutic
and sustained to release tensions we take
as fuel to our frenzies, the thirsts we slake.

Epsilon

I naught else matters in this moment, but that

naught else matters in this moment, but that
we are here, together. in unity
we find affinity in textures that
flow, the universe in community
with our presences sustains memory
for as long as we endure, sure of clear
skies and gentle rains, stains of pains washed free
to the trail to flow away, disappear
into the distance, what matters the most
is the serene envelope of peace we
fold ourselves in, sealed with gentle kiss, dosed
with the venom and elixir of free
will and the cure to sorrow and sad strife.
you, here with me. we have been given life.

II you, here with me. we have been given life

you, here with me. we have been given life
to share to care to dare to love to lust
and in this moment we fulfill that, rife
with affections and passions and the trust
that this is why we are here, our purpose
more than existence, per se, so we play
and press ever upwards in the circus
of this manifesting madness, we pray
to God who alone has authority
to criticize our performance in lieu
of the billions of sour grape souls that we
are surrounded by, their applause anew
for life, truth for truth, hope for acrobat.

III for life, truth for truth, hope for acrobat

for life, truth for truth, hope for acrobat
and audience alike is the pleasure
of exhilaration, death-defiance that
refreshes and revives our full measure
of our certainty that we can endure
the slings and arrows of our outrageous
misfortunes, reborn in raptures to cure
world weariness and doubt of courageous
moments, like a kiss, reaching out to bless
with a message of expression, loving
life and to communicate and confess
our affections and exuberance, bring
our continual rebirth, our fresh life,
faith that all will be as it should, midwife.

IIII faith that all will be as it should, midwife

faith that all will be as it should, midwife
to the memories and with practiced hands
you guide me to excitation to life
you bring that which in me once slept, the stands
to your own purpose. and welcome to wake,
to take the fill, you are, wont to swallow
in many ways, your primal thirst to slake
as you quench and wrench my awe to wallow
in the delight and depravity wet
with summoned, sudden sweat all consuming
while leaving us begging, bartering, set
against the colorless days and blooming
in hues of a spectrum we can compose.
fears are not for such as us, we propose.

V fears are not for such as us, we propose

fears are not for such as us, we propose
and dispose of ideas and dreams, settling
not for the easy, lazy paths suppose
to accept to avoid struggles, meddling
in the master plan of entropy, bright
and brisant our affection, harmony
with the celestial and the one sight
that fills us with wonder and thunder, free
to hold one another, experience
the sound of our heartbeats, they synchronize
as they were born to, sworn to, transcendence
and transfiguration, striking down lies
we were once taught (by blind men in the night)
to dispose of our clothes just out of sight.

VI to dispose of our clothes just out of sight

to dispose of our clothes just out of sight
for a stolen moment in laundry piles
much less comfortable than your bed, white
with the starched sheets and linens, but our smiles
are magnified by our careful deceits
as we make quick work of the marathon
we would have preferred, cured of our defeats
for the moment as we find sorrows gone
if only for now. we are gluttonous
and insatiable and every chance
that presents itself for our mutinous
conduct against authorities perchance
having forgot the solferino rose,
of those who would judge us for passion's throes.

VII of those who would judge us for passion's throes

of those who would judge us for passion's throes
consider that we alone are convict
for our sins, if such they are, and for those
who consider us lost, I must conflict
with their sphincteric minds, mesalliance
with zealous, jealous fools for whom the scent
of jasmine is a selfish reliance
on the words of cracked messengers, recent,
unrepentant self-anointed scornful
liars and buyers of the crowd's folly
in order to buy their own way, mournful
their followers, misguided equally
but of ignorance opposed to mob's flight
that nudge us towards a reckless delight.

VIII that nudge us towards a reckless delight

that nudge us towards a reckless delight,
the forces of rage and lost memories
that once danced in joy and ecstasies' night
born of a love and the shed sackcloth's breeze
where we contemplate the nature of soft
angels penetrated by the spires sprung
from loins of consented suitors, aloft
and seeking refuge in the cotton hung
as thinnest disguise and armor against
amorous intentions, tensions released
to be set again by caresses sensed
in six dimensions as the clock runs, priest
of the amotations, limits of night
touching and tumbling and fumbling in spite.

VIIII touching and tumbling and fumbling in spite

touching and tumbling and fumbling in spite
of our best intentions, mentioned to meet
the ritual requirements for light
courtship, belied by pounding blood and sweet
coitship, the necessary innocence,
naivete swept away in your arms, hands,
and tongue, sprung from Aphrodite's high sense
of low purposes, celebrated plans
incinerated: body heat approach
to Planck's number, warning lights to eyes blind
from the radiance of your sublime broach
of my desires when I see you, to find
the most interesting truths to preface
of the inappropriateness of place.

X of the inappropriateness of place

of the inappropriateness of place:
much debate, I hate to state we are not
proper in our pleasures here, no disgrace
hedonism with heroism caught
in our web of explorations, brought up
to the tip of the obelisk, you trace
sigils and runes of lost religions' cup
of sacral wine divine to your sweet face
as you draw out my seed and oaths in word
in languages not of this world, but learned
in a future, distant sphere where I heard
your name in a vision invoked and burned
into my flesh and soul, license of site
or time in which we feel the urgent right.

XI or time, in which we feel the urgent right.

or time, in which we feel the urgent right.
or place, in which we feel the need to bleed
in warm white or jasmine pink sacred rite
to consecrate our want or wish or need
as we make nerves flash in the electric
feels that twist our forms in celebration
a consecration of rude fluids thick
with sensual nourishment, foundation
for the spires that pierce you again, again,
and when you have recovered, once more to
bring light and lively charity, arcane
and holy in our pursuit, breathing new
zest in times of sorrows, whispering grace
to demonstrate our ardor and make case.

XII to demonstrate our ardor and make case

to demonstrate our ardor and make case
for our crucial copulation, action
against the storm of time and sad disgrace
that our species has not yet perfection
in their world, not like that I find when eyes
widen in awed awareness of our hearts,
extended as metaphor in the skies
and lies of poets and diplomats, parts
played for a moment's advantage in games
where there is, for us, no real victory
to be proud of, merely trivial frames
that do not affect lives or history.
we are here, together, for lovers' peace,
for the consummation and the release.

XIII for the consummation and the release

for the consummation and the release
from our contracts of Eden, the sentence
of sentience being death, we must cease
counting sands and band together penance
to be found in the most native of joys,
spinning our connections on a wheel hot
with your breath and touch, such as life employs
to make certain our conceits and feats sought
once for self-satisfaction now extend
the olive branch to a merged memory
where there are not words that one can pretend
capture the raptures of woke reverie
consumed as bread and wine as torments' cease
that leads boiling blood to satisfied peace.

XIIII that leads boiling blood to satisfied peace

that leads boiling blood to satisfied peace,
but what traces back our hearts to the war
wherein we find epic challenges please
our sense of having earned redemption, for
we need to feel deserving of our fate
as I have always sought to be worthy
of your majesty and beauty, your state
of excellence, inspiring naught earthly
praise and poetry, but also humbling
me, as said, "Seulement en face de Dieu"
ringing true as I bow and pray, mumbling
mantras and catechisms, stating true
my passions and unworthiness, in fact
naught else matters in this moment, but that.

naught else matters in this moment, but that
you, here with me. we have been given life
for life, truth for truth, hope for acrobat
faith that all will be as it should, midwife
fears are not for such as us, we propose
to dispose of our clothes just out of sight
of those who would judge us for passion's throes
that nudge us towards a reckless delight
touching and tumbling and fumbling in spite
of the inappropriateness of place
or time in which we feel the urgent right
to demonstrate our ardor and make case
for the consummation and the release
that leads boiling blood to satisfied peace.

Paragon

I That you have stood, in my heart and apart

That you have stood, in my heart and apart
from all others, girls and women forgot
as you entered my life, my loins and heart
are yours, yours alone, passions bought and brought
as sacrifice against the artifice
of pretenders and the vague candidates
who knew not of what they wished for in this.
there are none as perfect as you and fates
celebrate your quintessential essence,
bright and beautiful, wise and wonderful
in those things that matter most, your presence
is my evidence of God, bountiful
hope that you are an answer to prayers, far
from all other women, an avatar.

II from all other women, an avatar

from all other women, an avatar
shining bright and delightful, a divine
sparked by the necessity that there are
persons and things worth our worships' enshrine.
beyond my pale desires of my youth, you
stand as personification of love
in all its aspects, eros and the true
affection of romantic love, above
mere longing and the animal cravings
of a boy, unknowing of what he wants
when he feels the raw, consuming ravings
that seek to make feral delicate haunts
in soul cages of part Artemis, start
of dreams and desire, Aphrodite part.

III of dreams and desire, Aphrodite part

of dreams and desire, Aphrodite part
of the grand design, divinity cut
from stone and ether to lay for our heart
a semblance of our completion, the rut
of our primitive carnality, gripped
in the vise of contention, the mention
of our alliance and peace has me stripped
to my barest essence, an intention
to spend my days in harmonies with you
and my nights in a perfecting union
where we explore our limits to imbue
our universe with the blessed communion
that is the aggregate, and in both part
and parcel, divine and lust reservoir.

IIII And parcel, divine and lust reservoir

And parcel, divine and lust reservoir,
all things as mélange to the fantasies
that wake us, take us by our consents, for
we are at our greatest in unities
of thought and emotion and of action
as we fraction our lives for the traction
to seek pleasant purposes joined as one,
joy and celebration of life, friction
allowing us to move together, set
on a constant path to greater heaven
than found in pantomime pleasures, as wet
as they may be, but simulacra when
held against the perfect you, now clear cut
to fill me with the fever for your rut.

V to fill me with the fever for your rut

to fill me with the fever for your rut
there is nothing better than your kisses,
drawing out my soul that you may know what
pleases me, that I may please you, misses
and near-misses are hisses in the wind
grazing the target but the point denies
the purpose it was launched for, the thin-skinned
penetration and satisfying prize
of your sighs of comfort and completion,
transitory release to piece our peace
in one another's arms and bodies, won
wondering if we have time to increase
the moment's détente with one another
and reconciliation with the dark.

VI and reconciliation with the dark

and reconciliation with the dark
when the best sensations are in shadow,
rooted, undisputed connection, stark
as our need for one another, the glow,
the radiance and salience to lives
seeking a grip on reality, crisp
and penetrative, the blood of warm knives
that are invited to the slaughter, wisp
of light and the mossy floor of forest,
fortuitous bed for the passions led
away from civilization, we rest
as our most ancient ancestors when fed
and content, our peace can even abut
daemons of my mosaic soul, a cut.

VII daemons of my mosaic soul, a cut

daemons of my mosaic soul, a cut
of glass and sapphire, higher and the spire
disappears into the clouds below but
we are lost in the burnished afterfire,
glowing with improbable radiance
as our hypergolic hormones ignite
and light is within us, spilling out, dance
and seismic meanders, candors of sight
and sound and touch and taste, instinct and scent
like a forest after conflagration
has turned to ash the greatest, bright boughs spent
as fuel to measure heat in sweet ration
leaving only carbon burned, crystal dark
diamond in the temple of glass, the spark.

VIII diamond in the temple of glass, the spark

diamond in the temple of glass, the spark
is now captured in the gemstone facets,
against which the refractions will not mark
the barest water, daughter of tacit
remembrances, frozen in hot crystal
by the pressures of distant worlds beyond
the horizons of light in the distal
limits of amomancies that respond
to our unrelenting expressed belief
that love is of many spectra and shines
sometimes, sometimes, in frequencies' relief,
cartography of vineyards where the wines
sparkle in more manners, radiations
against which, other illuminations.

VIIII against which other illuminations

against which other illuminations
dim and flicker, we shine, divine, regent,
growing stronger as we bend damnations
to be resurrected by our advent.
the pieces fit, however we turn them,
making us a puzzle for the ages
as we smile and laugh at private jokes, from
last night and a decade ago, sages
of a personal philosophy, free
to explore or ignore as we see fit,
putting the pieces together to see
what the solution we get, spun to knit
while other romances, shade against moon
must be seen as lesser lights, stars at noon.

X Must be seen as lesser lights, stars at noon

Must be seen as lesser lights, stars at noon,
these flickers of rubies that fall from lips,
primed and prepared to receive very soon
enough, offering of release for hips
that will in due time draw me in to coit
with savage tenderness and a just trace
of the spirit awakening to adroit
nature of your guidance, as in your face,
a rosary of meditation, sprung
from the stray thoughts we capture in our hearts
as we chase the clouds with lips and with tongue,
tracing shadow outlines against the parts
such that I close my eyes in nictations.
in blinding me you have been temptations.

XI in blinding me you have been temptations

in blinding me you have been temptations
to all senses I acknowledged, angel
and temptress and sweet sacred seductions
burning deep inside me as a faithful
brand. marking your ownership in lustful
pride and patience, the precipice tested
and eventually defeated, full
of terror no more, we soar beyond pull
of grave gravity, our confidence grown
every measure, treasure and reward
for my faith and purpose, paramour shown
more than mere lover, the most crucial chord
played between us, the melodious tune
to my oath to serve love incarnate, strewn.

XII to my oath to serve love incarnate, strewn

to my oath to serve love incarnate, strewn
like hastily discarded clothes, from door
to bed, paving the path to sacred rune
marked upon your thigh that I find valor
in this surrender, slipped in steady glide
inside with pride and urgent pleasures set
to summon endorphins, your legs spread wide
to receive me into your vault of wet
delights, joy our vision, yesterday dark
with purposeless sorrows, we celebrate
victories and efforts against the mark
left by others' sins and judgements, our fait
accompli accomplished against the trials,
past as reservations, as denials.

XIII past as reservations, as denials

past as reservations, as denials,
as we have no need of the forsaken
stakes we bet against in substance, the styles
of our perceptions, masquerade taken
to pass in company unworthy, proud
of who we are but seeking yet to prove
our virtue and value beyond the crowd
that presses on all sides but in, we move
in intersecting lines, until we enter
one another's space, tracing our penance
to make silhouette of shadows, center
and sustained, paid as a joyful presence
two in one, revolt against false cycles
in the face of confessing disciples.

XIIII in the face of confessing disciples

in the face of confessing disciples.
the scripture is undone, the word is here
to make us incarnations of rivals
for the milkweed religions held so near
by those who lost that we are created
in the image of a passionate God,
prone to fire, tears and jealousy, fated
to have Their doubts to the prototype, flawed
as it is, but striving to live, break out
of the shallow grave we dig ourselves to
shovel dirt over us while we breathe, doubt
shouted down in the desert, this is true:
I will be grateful from the very start
that you have stood, in my heart and apart.

XV That you have stood, in my heart and apart (diadem)

That you have stood, in my heart and apart
from all other women, an avatar
of dreams and desire, Aphrodite part
and parcel, divine and lust reservoir
to fill me with the fever for your rut
and reconciliation with the dark
daemons of my mosaic soul, a cut
diamond in the temple of glass, the spark
against which other illuminations
must be seen as lesser lights, stars at noon,
in blinding me you have been temptations
to my oath to serve love incarnate, strewn
past as reservations, as denials
in the face of confessing disciples.

Marathon

I Through the heavy evening and sweet night

Through the heavy evening and sweet night
when the light fails, we do not abandon
our passions. You have been held out of sight
and out of reach for too long, and sudden
sustained opportunity, unity
draws us together, your temple takes in
my stone and seethe, taking community
in our merged flesh and fancies, porous skin
making way for the kneeling and sealing
of vows and vindications, performing
in our expected roles, but exceeding
expectations of pleasure, measuring
our union in wet frictions, and fragrant
we coit like creatures feral and flagrant.

II we coit like creatures feral and flagrant

we coit like creatures feral and flagrant,
sounding our guttural excitations,
and eloquent, coin of our loins unspent,
we barter hungers, manifestations
of a yet deeper need that we would feed
without hesitation, any regard
for the aftermath we leave as we bleed,
souls and bodies, torn apart to be scarred
by the stigmata of the romantiques,
expressing the dimensions of our lives
in dances, entwined, ancient semantics
tearing apart the barriers, archives
of a prophecy, panic in the night,
rustles in the undergrowth, glowing bright.

III rustles in the undergrowth, glowing bright

rustles in the undergrowth, glowing bright,
as your eyes did when I first fed on you,
drawing strength and fulfillment in forthright
admiration, the taste of your gates' dew
guiding me to seek deeper and in time
to sip the nectar of your chalice, sweet
and floral, like your dreams, a flavor prime
and primordial, whispering compleat
surrender and victory, as you press
me against you, your thighs tensing to ride
sparks, an electrification to bless
your most sacred form with warmth from inside
to provide us a sanctuary, bent
keen with our preoccupation, vagrant.

IIII keen with our preoccupation, vagrant

keen with our preoccupation, vagrant
forms seeking warm recompense for the touch.
hand on hand. fingertips tracing fragrant
zones bloom the orchid and prepare it such
to receive the stalk of my manhood, pressed
between all manner of lips to find soft
wet reception, folding emboldened quest
of peace and release, holding skies aloft
on an arched back, stacking the sensations
of the consecrated consummations
we renew in our giddy joy, rations
repeatedly shared faith and foundations
as we bend and twist in our atonements
in the forms we take to mold to moments.

V in the forms we take to mold to moments

in the forms we take to mold to moments
we are magnified and revealed, facet
by facet, aspect by aspect, intense
as your inner pulse finds me and we set
a rhythm of blood and primitive grip
that swallows me to hold me, minuet
of unsubtle fury, steps that will skip
from heartbeat to heartbeat in pirouette
ravenous as we improvise our moves
and smile, radiant, with the full measure
of this found gemstone in the dirt. this proves
that there is more to life than the treasure
apparent to those seeking what is caught,
set aside for the slide of membranes, hot.

VI set aside for the slide of membranes, hot

set aside for the slide of membranes, hot
and constantly in motion emotions
intensified and undenied when caught
in infinite webs kiss and words frozen,
emphatic empathetic transmissions
on a wavelength carried in lipstick red,
scarlet, ruddy, ruby and emissions
in the warm white wine taken in to spread
the gospel of passions performed to raise
the fires of desires higher than closed eyes
can imagine, transfixed by the rare blaze
that licks at your heart as I did your thighs
in seeking our shared sustenance to dance
with blood and craving, seizing the intense.

VII with blood and craving, seizing the intense

with blood and craving, seizing the intense,
wrestling with your fervent, fevered rapture,
straining to feed the fires knowledge and sense
amazed by the tantalizing touch, pure
and defiled, you smiled, you lay in my arms
and shared the heat, sweet and satisfying
we extend moments of merger in charms
light reflecting off our sweat, edifying
our tutelage of what pleases us most
in experiences and empathies
collected to respect and protect, host
of our sweet memories and fantasies
as we dare to dream and dance the gavotte,
the sublime, subtle divinity, taut.

VIII the sublime, subtle divinity, taut

the sublime, subtle divinity, taut
the lips that will measure seizure and sigh
as I tease your pink meringues and lay hot
hands against the curve of your buttock, thigh,
and essential sweet folds that guard and guide
the welcomed lover inside to dive deep
and draw sustaining friction from inside
as we kiss and draw ragged breaths that keep
us pumped like a bellows, incandescent
furnaces of intimate expression
as the anvil hammered, iridescent
visions, spectra evolving possession
is nine inches of the law, auspicious
tautology, welcome and delicious.

VIIII Tautology, welcome and delicious

Tautology, welcome and delicious
the repetitive thrust and drive that finds
us touching ever more inches of us,
feeling the curves and swerves and nerves, the kinds
of truths we did not expect this close to
the periphery of our inner eyes,
placing and displacing rigid heat through
the barest manipulations and prize
predations of our prey, we pray this day
our daily thread of conquered fears and tears
wept in every conceivable melee
of lovers' purpose and practice that nears
the summits of Olympus, gods' control
to take in trace nibbles and gorge on soul.

X to take in trace nibbles and gorge on soul

to take in trace nibbles and gorge on soul,
we are scavengers and the hunting hawks
released to find the running target, role
of the feast to be taken in like flocks
of tasty angels, giving up their light,
their very substance to satisfy needs
of the mortals melting into the night
where the robust writhing betrays our seeds,
feeding us our own hungers like harpies
in a frenzy to catch and capture meat
to fill our metaphoric bellies, tease
and totality offered and complete
to the sacred side of love, Lazarus
and antithesis of it, rapturous.

XI And antithesis of it, rapturous

And antithesis of it, rapturous
in our all-consuming focus, magic
woven of the needs that will not discuss
their agenda, blinders on and tragic
memory faded in the serenades
that sing with your whispers and tender touch,
a spur to cure hesitancy, charades
in an eloquent silence that is such
a cacophony to senses seeking
solace inside you, the sweet heat swallows
all and greedily demands more, speaking
with an untentative tongue that follows
lips, purging urgency, out of control
and pure, sure of our merry moment's role.

XII And pure, sure of our merry moment's role

And pure, sure of our merry moment's role
in the fallen temples of temptation,
tearing us asunder in thunder roll
in the aftermath of lightning, ration
of the irrational mind, animals
ravenous and ready, steady on path
to find our feed for greedy mandibles
and the gluttony of redemptive wrath
as we find our transfiguration in
wet wonders of our transport, releasing
unconscious sounds of luxury within
radius of our reaches, unceasing
shenanigans serving our devotion
infinite boundaries of emotion.

XIII infinite boundaries of emotion

infinite boundaries of emotion
shattered in our scattering fire we catch
our skin from fires within escaping one
way or another and another. latch
sprung and the egress opens to our wills
and whims and we take gleeful advantage
of the opportunity and take fills
of our infinite lusts, our core coeur rage
spreading like your legs and lips to welcome
me to the closest thing to heaven set
in this, my universe, where you seldom
fail to cure my ennui, the pirouette
of your dance mesmerizes, explosion,
wait forever, both poison and potion.

XIIII Wait forever, both poison and potion

Wait forever, both poison and potion
courses through our veins, the stains of bloodlust
burning us alive, an immolation
that steams and streams in screams of draw and thrust,
churning the coals to heat beyond measure
frantic romantiques leaving fingerprints
as we clutch at tension and the leisure
of the moment of release, queen and prince
to a new world order, reigning, straining
to find the light and the elegance born
in the perfect fit that flutters, staining
our universe with reds and pinks, and sworn
to rule our unity with perfect right
through the heavy evening and sweet night.

XV Through the heavy evening and sweet night (diadem)

Through the heavy evening and sweet night
we coit like creatures feral and flagrant,
rustles in the undergrowth, glowing bright,
keen with our preoccupation, vagrant
in the forms we take to mold to moments
set aside for the slide of membranes, hot
with blood and craving, seizing the intense,
the sublime, subtle divinity, taut
tautology, welcome and delicious
to take in trace nibbles and gorge on soul
and antithesis of it, rapturous
and pure, sure of our merry moment's role.
infinite boundaries of emotion
wait forever, both poison and potion.

go down on

your flower is pretty, tasty besides,
I will take my fill until you call break
as you are so overwhelmed by the rides
you undertake for your bright passions' sake
setting the rhythm and the path as you
clutch my hair and stare into nothingness,
lost in the heat and sensation, now through
your flesh into your blood and heart, you press
your body against my ravenous mouth
that draws air and sweetness in the pattern
of your burning, churning and straddled south,
holding on for dear life, feral lantern
in the infrared, sorrow is destroyed
petals hide nothing but your joy, employed.

petals hide nothing but your joy, employed
as a defense against my insistence
that I will win the pleasure centers, void
of all restraints, feint the taint, persistence,
leverage, beverage for this banquet
lapped in joyful ignition of the fire
that burns deep inside, stoked and stroked to sweat
sweetest aroma of delight, inspire
as your erectile tissues meet my graze
and I gaze on you with wonder as gasps
and moans make vocabulary to praise
my ministrations, your spasmodic grasps
are all the encouragement I need, guides
to please you with kisses and the smooth glides.

III to please you with kisses and the smooth glides

to please you with kisses and the smooth glides
lips and fingertips across sensitive
tissues, teased and pleased until the divides
between us melt and run, the tentative
explorations lead to discovery
disconcerting loss of inhibitions
a tidal wave rising, recovery
of your senses washed away, positions
shifted and awareness drifted like sand
in the desert storm, warm and violent,
you shake, take refuge in a wonderland
of release without cease as your silent
screams find voice as I break restraint, destroyed,
of my emboldening tongue, now enjoyed.

IIII of my emboldening tongue, now enjoyed

of my emboldening tongue, now enjoyed,
I speak a haptic language, loving words
calling you to rest and trust my deployed
expressions, the light speech of hummingbirds
transmitted in touch and bold tremulous
tracings with the outline of runes in wet
and heated conversation to discuss
where these moments fit in the scheme we set
for our lives, together, the melting wax
of the candles that mark our mortal span
smooths the succulent moments that relax
the stain and strain of our days of our plan,
communicating with the wetting word
as expression of affections explored.

V as expression of affections explored

as expression of affections explored
in delicious study of the fountains
of vivacious affections, unignored
the way you whisper my name, soft mountains
and their tensing pink meringue tips echo
your sentiments and sweet encouragements,
cascading down to me to let me know
how close you are to little death, events
rippling as I hold fast, last forever
if that is your need and feed to heavens
opened to allow my prayers, so clever,
and ministrations to your unleaven
bread and wine divine, communion's appease
by a suitor eager to please and tease.

VI by a suitor eager to please and tease

by a suitor eager to please and tease,
dead serious and happily joyful
in celebrations as we seek to please
one another, ripe and ribald, gleeful,
and set to explode with ten thousand sparks
of incandescent nerves, alive with soul
and tissue, your sharp nails leave sacred marks
on neck and shoulders as I swallow whole
your desires, fires kindled in religious
fervor, the false prophets revealed in this,
my Shibboleth before your grace, pious
in my worship, respectful extremis
with lips full and moist, offering restored,
eyes gleaming, your body screaming accord.

VII eyes gleaming, your body screaming accord

eyes gleaming, your body screaming accord
with all unspoken agreements, assent
to be canvas for each masterpiece scored
in textures of a kitten's respect, sent
as an archangel to salvage savage
residual emotions buried long
beneath the debris of the average,
channeling us to an uncertain song
played on wet frets of erotic tensions
plagiarized romances, dances tepid
and insipid in limp limpids, mentions
without context, love made in the trepid
tropics, not revealed in an earnest ease
with brisant bravado, gripped thighs to seize.

VIII with brisant bravado, gripped thighs to seize

with brisant bravado, gripped thighs to seize
to hold me tight against you, late night fights
the rising storm of warm passions, to freeze
no more the mind and soul and flesh, delights
overpowered Heracles, stampeding
up and down your spine in time with my kiss,
gentle dental stimulation feeding
my lust and your lust and our melded bliss
that trickles like honeysuckle nectar
on a hot Los Angeles night, cocktail
with the scent of night blooming jasmine, far
from the Mississippi coast, the new trail
to break away, now seeking to be free
on more exploratory probity.

VIIII on more exploratory probity

on more exploratory probity
discovery is more than mere purpose
to propose for adventure. sanity,
vanity, and curiosity, rose
and dandelion, now blowing away
in the faintest of breezes as seizes
your whim and fantasies, the heartfelt play
that translates to an ancient tongue, teases
a revelation in torn veils and sails
that wave in the horse latitudes as we
stroke our oars to overcome many fails
marked in lost ships and lonely hips, debris
on the road to the grand consecration
in your sacred temple of temptation.

X in your sacred temple of temptation

in your sacred temple of temptation
there is no more room for the acolytes
who filled the lonely nights, hesitation
to sacrifice their very lives in rites
as ancient as lost Ka-Latil, standing
silent beneath the sands of time, perfect
and forgotten. forsaken, remanding
legends to ghosts in the mirrors, neglect
a passion I reject, I genuflect
on the graven image of you burned in
to my mind and touch, passion and respect
marking an indelible idol of sin
sanctified in my brave controversy,
the veils parted by my breath, no mercy.

XI the veils parted by my breath, no mercy

the veils parted by my breath, no mercy
is asked or given, as I dive between
thighs I know so well that tis courtesy
alone that requires they are to be seen
for even in the darkness they are most
beautiful and I focus all ardor
to ensure you feel every ghost I host
in toasting you with your own vintage, for
have no doubt, I do not want to be where
I cannot take my fill of your passions,
in greedy gathering of your most fair
flavour, savour of my taste and missions
to find evidence of God, proved notion
as small deaths roll like waves on an ocean.

XII as small deaths roll like waves on an ocean

as small deaths roll like waves on an ocean
I cling for my life, amplifying greed
for depths of eroticism, potion
to raise the dead for yet another bleed
of the white wine as transfusion of love
in the near term, having lost track tonight
of how many times, but Lola thereof
can retire the field or reclaim her right
if she possesses you and the Duke takes
my form to seek to exceed our excess
in finding sweeter feast and undertakes
to wake Endymion to give caress,
turning river into mighty ocean
to pound your shores with hungry erosion.

XIII to pound your shores with hungry erosion

to pound your shores with hungry erosion
I would rise up, a tsunami to crash
to you, overturning all emotion
as the primal urge to surge and to smash
overwhelms me, personification
of winds and waters and sky, I am not
some simpleton seeking satiation
but a living agent of change, soul caught
in the perfecting wheel, resurrection
in the immortality carried deep
to burst forth in blinding glory, flection
of the middle way, where grey is gold, weep
for unwoken, I dispel emotion,
of your final doubts of my devotion.

XIIII of your final doubts of my devotion?

of your final doubts of my devotion?
I will lay here, I will stay here, to clear
the ambiguities in my notion
that I am bound to you both far and near.
we are entangled, the past is mangled!
we heal as a single beautiful thing
redeemed even by carnal acts, tangled
limbs and my feasting between your shining,
graceful legs, a faceful of your essence
my reward for my suit and persistence
as we lay here, a merged purged scourged presence
as I redefine tongue-lash in instance:
no regret, our river of sweat wet guides.
your flower is pretty, tasty besides.

XV your flower is pretty, tasty besides (diadem)

your flower is pretty, tasty besides,
petals hide nothing but your joy, employed
to please you with kisses and the smooth glides
of my emboldening tongue, now enjoyed
as expression of affections explored
by a suitor eager to please and tease,
eyes gleaming, your body screaming accord
with brisant bravado, gripped thighs to seize
on more exploratory probity
in your sacred temple of temptation
the veils parted by my breath, no mercy
as small deaths roll like waves on an ocean
to pound your shores with hungry erosion
of your final doubts of my devotion.

Set Upon

I I am overwhelmed by your rare beauty,

I am overwhelmed by your rare beauty,
prisoner of my own desire and fate
to wait for the next bardo, the duty
withheld to follow the flow past the gate
of one's own desires to find redemption
in a kiss or subtle gesture to set
in motion the emotions, exemption
to the logical whim, criminal bet
on the higher purposes and postures
of infinite variations, regret
and pride, bound in syntax, the imposture
of a prophet upon the parapet
calling out their holy call to heart's arms,
taken hostage and ransom to your charms.

II taken hostage and ransom to your charms

taken hostage and ransom to your charms,
I am resigned to my fortune and fate,
to look the other way when the alarms
are sounded, confounded to the frustrate
as Alexander to Gordius, caught
in the knot that shot me down, a single
swipe of steel to sever the binding thought
that there is destiny afoot, tingle
and tremors, the rhapsody of our skin
spoken of as a single entity
where exposed nerves swerve and curve to begin
the dance, eyes to eyes, new identity
established as you teach me unity
even in the calm hours you sleep, tutee.

III even in the calm hours you sleep, tutee

even in the calm hours you sleep, tutee
to tutee, we seek the true tutelage,
both eager for greater truth and the free
exchange of ideas and fluids, pillage
prize and shared in repetitions of joy
as we mark our days and nights, affections
affecting our every corner, coy
with our confessions, our recollections
of past lovers and liars in our spheres,
snuggling closer to share heat and defeat
the scrimshaw memories of pagan peers
to our religion of devotion, sweet
is our communion, past wards and alarms
to all your secrets, the smile that disarms.

IIII to all your secrets, the smile that disarms

to all your secrets, the smile that disarms,
a pleasant face to shield your pain, you seek
defense, retribution for all the harms
visited on you by callous who pique
our rages, for cages they trapped you in
for their own purposes as they told you
this is what you want, as they haunt the thin
truth that is easily dismissed, untrue
persuasions, not in your own interests
to follow their lead, need for company
makes lemmings of us all, fair Icarus
fell from self-deception, accompany
perfected self-definition, unfurled
peace, ultimate weapon against this world

V peace, ultimate weapon against this world

peace, ultimate weapon against this world
that can seem and be so brutal, the sword
does not cure the sword but validates hurled
hatred. We are creatures of love the cord
to heaven is strong and we sing songs bright
and inspiring of our connections, true
to our Creator, we seek words of light
and love, reaching for skies where angels flew
to in constant chaos of the heavens,
indifferent to us, it is for us
to soothe and protect one another, yens
to be away from silence, to discuss
the iron of life by the withered sedge
in which every corner has sharp edge.

VI in which every corner has sharp edge

in which every corner has sharp edge
best to stay to the center and place me
between you and harm, it is sacred pledge
to stand against the storms that batter free
souls to the limits of heart's survival,
the agony of this harsh existence
as the winds and lashing rains' revival
come about to shout you down, persistence
of a universe without the limits
or boundaries that we inherited
wherein we are called to love, pith and pits,
succulent feasting, on each other, bed
and post, against those that tear down our world
and seeks to cut us down to futile, furled.

VII and seeks to cut us down to futile, furled

and seeks to cut us down to futile, furled
bannerettes for the armies of passion,
shock troop Amomancers, around them curled
the nightfall dancers whose high position
we leap from in despair when we feel lost,
that the fall is worth the freedom from tears
wept in silent solitude, bitter cost
of holding to our own standards, the jeers
of the crushing crowds of cowards caught up
in their own limited definitions
in language of predatory hookup
and the forget-me-now expeditions
that make no exceptions for earnest fledge
afterthoughts, shot to pieces on the ledge.

VIII afterthoughts, shot to pieces on the ledge

afterthoughts, shot to pieces on the ledge
to deny the lie that spawned the moment
we might regret if we were honest, hedge
of the invested time and love, current
karma against the craps table, the odds
breaking us, feeling alone by your choice
when you choose indifference to the gods
of lovers and dreamers, using your voice
to commit blasphemy and doubt the life
that waits for you when paired with lover's touch
to fulfill the faith bound in a dream rife
with the pleasures and treasures that are such
you find abundance, unlike those who play
of the highest places, wasting away.

VIIII of the highest places, wasting away

of the highest places, wasting away
is the pretend Prometheus, crying
out in torment for the pecking and flay
at the command of fading gods dying
as their authoritarian times end
and mortals step out of shadows and cold
to find warmth in fire and desire, to mend
and cauterize our wounds with heat and bold
gestures to draw together in our time
with kind caresses and tender kisses
as we reach for more mortality, prime
numbers in divisive universes
that offer equation that recovers
for the ambiguities of lovers.

X for the ambiguities of lovers

for the ambiguities of lovers
there is no certain relief to the thought,
a personal demon that discovers
your Achilles heel, your will has been bought
by years of insecurities handed
us by malicious ministers of fear
that do not want us content but branded
by symbols of our discontent held near
in an illusion of safety, as wards
against the imaginary devils
that will play the fool and the knave of swords
to jinx our reading to skew the levels
of our ascendency, against the sway,
that hide their cards and karma, so to play.

XI that hide their cards and karma, so to play

that hide their cards and karma, so to play,
the gamblers mistrust the game making lame
the dancers and divines that seek the way
to place their two mites now in Pascal's name
caring nothing for the fate of others,
they mock the higher love we are seeking
to the evolution of hearts, mothers
and fathers, and heirs to sunrise peeking
through the proud clouds diffusing the shadows
we cannot cast to tell the sun from sky
as we taste our time and tale to oppose
those who have not found or held but deny
all that is beautiful and discovers
their grim game where the loser recovers.

XII their grim game where the loser recovers

their grim game where the loser recovers
is played with marked cards by the falsest gods
who give no thought to what they do, lovers
in name alone, for there is no love, nods
to the darkest of spirits is your prayer
that you say in the mirror, Narcissus
salutes you but you are unworthy, rare
the introspective romantic witness
bears the evidence and the shame for lies
told in the previous lives left behind
like cicadas shedding their shells and prize
of metamorphosis includes their bind
to their own perfidy, their third eye blind
by the side of the road, now left behind.

XIII by the side of the road, now left behind

by the side of the road, now left behind
all others who hovered for their feasting,
carrion flies seeking just their assigned
niche in the menagerie of screaming
gutter bugs, the purposes in their place
is to serve as impediment to light,
blocking the sun and the air to disgrace
and defile all that they can, bitter blight
on all that is and should be, the debris
of misery and corruptors of joy
that, in their hands is nothing, entropy,
no mysteries or wonder, they destroy.
the tracest ascension of the soul, grind
to stumble in the most distant dark, blind.

XIIII to stumble in the most distant dark, blind

to stumble in the most distant dark, blind
is the fate of the dead that cannot tell
that they are finished, and we are assigned
a hopeful ascendency, birthing spell
of all manner of the antithesis
of Pandora's minions, hope and mercy,
a fresh and eternal hypothesis
to the virtue of God and angels, see
them bringing light in the dark corners set
in the deepest rooms of the soul, we voice
one another's true names as sobriquet,
carrying our own definition, choice
in freedom we are heirs to, a duty
I am overwhelmed by, your rare beauty,

XV I am overwhelmed by your rare beauty (diadem)

I am overwhelmed by your rare beauty,
taken hostage and ransom to your charms
even in the calm hours you sleep, tutee
to all your secrets, the smile that disarms.
peace, ultimate weapon against this world
in which every corner has sharp edge
and seeks to cut us down to futile, furled
afterthoughts, shot to pieces on the ledge
of the highest places, wasting away
for the ambiguities of lovers
that hide their cards and karma, so to play
their grim game where the loser recovers
by the side of the road, now left behind
to stumble in the most distant dark, blind.

Come Upon

I out of nowhere you entered my somewhere

out of nowhere you entered my somewhere,
with unusual hoopla, setting pace
with horns and drums, the explosive fanfare
and fireworks for an Olympian race
at least, that is how it sounded to me
when I heard your voice, and my heart awoke
from a seemingly eternal sleep, free
to dream of infinite fields, masterstroke
of celestial artists, elegant
angel to visit me with her presence,
dropping me to my knees in awe to grant
revelation of potential pleasance.
you were not expected but, joy abound,
even though I was lost, found common ground.

II even though I was lost, found common ground

even though I was lost, found common ground
with you, our hearts synchronize to our dreams
and we are pulled from sorrow into found
ecstasies, as we lay together, seams
all but invisible to us, your kiss
connects me to a cosmic minuet,
a dance best in a horizontal bliss
with only music of our sighs to set
us on an endless path, everlasting
and consuming me in necessary
reveries of life, the daydreams casting
their hooks ever deeper in my soul, free
to seek a new horizon, to build rare
where we could create a new nature, fair.

III where we could create a new nature, fair

where we could create a new nature, fair
and verdant, planting seeds for the futures
we want to live in, to give to time, share
with those who forgot their dreams, the tutors
of lessons to which we pay attention
as if it means our very lives, wonder
of the universe drifting in tension
within our hearts and minds, down and under
rippling sheets where beats our hearts to a rhythm
synchronized to our lovemaking, kissing
and caressing with light now a prism
through which passes our visions, a blessing
of perceptions, limitless sight and sound
and abundant, as are your virtues, bound.

IIII and abundant, as are your virtues, bound

and abundant, as are your virtues, bound
to you by life experiences, well
founded and sublime establishments, sound
judgement earned while visiting sky and hell,
where we learn truths that in the middle way
are not afforded us, bright lights, bruises,
and panoply of sights and sounds that sway
perceptions of good and evil, uses
us as the hosts of parasitic thought
that plays scaffold to the stage, our façade
built upon more than thin air, we are not
uncomplex beings, ignorance outlawed
through trial and many errors, we must lope
to one another in a sense of hope.

V to one another in a sense of hope

to one another in a sense of hope.
we bind ourselves, the passion and respect
we share amplifies our contentment, trope
and new expressions of what we expect
from the genesis of our story, told
in crisp scrimshaw on the frozen beaches
where we breathed misting airs in bitter cold
but bracing evaluations, breaches
of our imperfect armors of our hearts
where we are pierced in a fierce entrapment,
brought down by the venom of Cupid's darts
but not as trophy this time, nourishment
and sustainment, a shared annexation,
the wonder that you are, revelation.

VI the wonder that you are, revelation

the wonder that you are, revelation
to eyes bordering on faded, jaded
by experience of past relation,
battered, scattered thoughts now serenaded
by the harmonies of awakening
to new and fair possibilities, born
of the essence of our prophecy, sing
the songs of minstrels and trouvere, the scorn
of defeatism come from tepid brandy,
the mishandling of delight, the banquet
brought down by churlish manners, we bandy
words and mock our own country etiquette
losing sight of the flavor of true hope,
to the beginning of all things, the scope.

VII to the beginning of all things, the scope

to the beginning of all things, the scope
of our relationship has gone from friend
to lover, to both, yet an allotrope
of all things anticipated, hoped, end
and beginning, all between, all beyond
and dimensions of feelings and senses.
I wish you could see what I see now spawned
from random encounter, our defenses
melted and reformed around not just my
heart, but the twain, a symbiosis formed
by the needs and desires of both the sky
and the fire and the earth, the iceberg warmed
to make rain and tears, signification
of rebirth, of a better elation.

VIII of rebirth, of a better elation

of rebirth, of a better elation,
of an epic tale of paramours born
in the heat to sow a deeper sation
in the fields of Arbol, Nazarites shorn
of hair and purpose, clinging to pillars
to topple all that people think they know
but have but guessed from their caterpillar
experiences. Wings, they cannot grow
without a time of chrysalis, rebirth
and the emergence into gloried flight
to demonstrate your evolution, Earth
is no longer your home, the stars now light
your ascendency, on this very day
you lightened my soul and made straight the way.

VIIII you lightened my soul and made straight the way

you lightened my soul and made straight the way
to heavens, to the wonders of waking
in the morning with purpose and to stay
blessed by entangled heart and limbs, making
my life make sense for the first time ever,
the demons diminish and now are called
only for their antics when their clever
perversions please you (and they do), the sprawled
calling of the satyrs to bring a heat
beyond the sacred dance of sacraments,
for there are times we all seek sweet
surrender for our own dark atonements,
ways to the nurture of our passions' plays
I would travel for the rest of my days,

X I would travel for the rest of my days

I would travel for the rest of my days,
barefoot and homeless, to seek your blessing,
despite the years since you cast me out, ways
parted and the home we started? missing
the cohesion of our synergy, lost
was the respect and fallen idols lay
about the temples of the tempests, crossed
and trampled, no more laughter or love play
once the base words left your lips and I fell,
fell into a hell unrelenting, pain
you cannot comprehend as a cracked shell
remained of the man, standing in the rain
to catch the thunder and the lightning's flay,
seeking to extend and amplify sway.

XI seeking to extend and amplify sway

seeking to extend and amplify sway
over the outcomes of the rolled dice, price
paid in blood and flesh, ripped and torn away
to feel like a martyr, the slice and splice,
flayed alive when treasuring for no more
the continuance of sentient thought
but the moment of emotion, the pour
of brandywine, memory and just what
we were countenancing, dancing barefoot
on a wooden floor we could not conceive
was so distant and different we put
miles and decades between us, to believe
that we are deserving of love and praise,
that you hold now over me, as I gaze.

XII that you hold now over me, as I gaze

that you hold now over me, as I gaze
in mind mesmerized, on your naked form.
the subtle curve of your hips, now ablaze
with the fires of a furnace that is warm
enough to raise to red glow the shaft iron
seeking its place between your slender thighs,
the hypergolic fluids of the lion
and his sacred vessel ignite and rise
in a column of plasma to set fire
to the world and all in it, light and heat
making sweet the bitterness of the pyre
upon which we were discarded, defeat
conquered and charging the most ancient gate
into futures with a sense of the great.

XIII into futures with a sense of the great

into futures with a sense of the great
possibilities unleashed by our touch
as we explore in all ways, immolate
of ourselves to the infinite heart such
that we are living avatars aflame
and writhing in the blaze of our pleasures,
sharing all that we possess in a frame,
penetrations and consuming measures
of arousals and deaths in clasping grasps
to pull us closer and more completely
into each other as urgency gasps
and wails and moans, as you did, most sweetly
mere moments ago and in coming state,
possibilities for our future fate.

XIIII possibilities for our future fate.

possibilities for our future fate.
infinite and obstinate, we become
what we will when afforded to equate
love and power as they merge, overcome,
and establish themselves a newer state
of being, seeing with unclouded eyes
all that lays before us, hope to negate
the failed flying machine that crashed and dies
without ever more than an illusion
of the skies, a prize for token takings
with drumbeat promise to spark confusion
in those who want to find heroic things.
in perfect time to my imperfect prayer,
out of nowhere, you entered my somewhere,

XV out of nowhere you entered my somewhere (diadem)

out of nowhere you entered my somewhere,
even though I was lost, found common ground
where we could create a new nature, fair
and abundant, as are your virtues, bound
to one another in a sense of hope.
the wonder that you are, revelation
to the beginning of all things, the scope
of rebirth, of a better elation,
you lightened my soul and made straight the way
I would travel for the rest of my days,
seeking to extend and amplify sway
that you hold now over me, as I gaze
into futures with a sense of the great
possibilities for our future fate.

Settle On

I accepting not what was offered, in taste

accepting not what was offered, in taste,
but flavors we seek, tweaking destiny
with every sip, nip, or nibble we graced
with our satiety, our very free
rejoicing in our gluttony, the full
belly that tells us we have feasted well,
we pick and choose and ultimately cull
precisely what pleases us, flavors gel
as they slide across our lips, hypnosis
and the familiar trace of jasmine
and iron as we play our way, gnosis
from the blood and flesh, hearty companion
to sounds of love, responsibilities
of all the pleasant possibilities.

II of all the pleasant possibilities

of all the pleasant possibilities,
you are the one that I admire the most,
proud that you chose me to share your pretties
and darkest edges, sacramental toast
and prayer to the coming religion built
upon our satin scriptures, bandied hot
between barter and provocation, spilt
in warm white wine and saliva, gavotte
and the dance we follow in, then we lead
as the pounding in our blood matches bed
and the famished feast as we bleed the seed
of our consuming spirit, as we said
on more than one occasion, feast and taste
when we know there is fresh ambrosia, chaste.

III when we know there is fresh ambrosia, chaste

when we know there is fresh ambrosia, chaste
to the vintner's pull, the perfect bottle
opened to once again drink, measured haste
swallowing in appreciative sips,
the taste and texture turns to colors, heat,
and the sound of redemptive pulse in us,
feeling without seeing, hearing sound sweet
that is transmitted in the friction plus
the soft murmurations that are wordless
but communicate the gist of the kissed
covenants, the flavour and nothing less
than your spirit and heart that do not freeze
to the corruption of the low degrees.

IIII to the corruption of the low degrees

to the corruption of the low degrees
we rise to walk on the brackish waters
in which so many surrender, disease
and drowning to be their fates, the daughters
and sons of failed riddles and the mistakes
made and never recovered from, the loss
that became a pattern, an habit, breaks
broken and turned to glass in the dry gloss
that only simulates stimulations.
the false facades that make us uncertain
of the visions we have as vocation
allowed to rule lives, behind the curtain
where we, eventually rejected,
where we are malnourished and neglected.

V where we are malnourished and neglected

where we are malnourished and neglected
we will be loved and filled; all our needs met
in common press to make sure we are fed,
comforted in times of sorrow, we'll set
our course by our best interests, growing
stronger with time and the experience,
shared in our perfecting embrace, knowing
that tomorrow is never promised, hence
we will make the most of the moments we
have and find our way, both brave and brazen,
seekers of truth, rejoicing to be free
and liberated as we emblazon
the stars themselves, rescued with verve and nerve
from a false sense that we do not deserve.

VI from a false sense that we do not deserve

from a false sense that we do not deserve
to be content, or even happy, strike
back in rage and resentment to preserve
your ego and your spirit, not unlike
the struggle to emerge from the cocoon
that was meant to be spider's grim larder,
we struggle in vain, a tone to attune
to a necessity to fight harder,
hard enough to break our bonds and fly free,
making mythologies and mysteries
of the forgotten crypt where slipped the key
through cracks that doom so many histories
to be tragedies of starving hearts, led
to taste the nectar of Olympus, fed.

VII to taste the nectar of Olympus, fed

to taste the nectar of Olympus, fed
to the deities to nourish their strength
(and egos), sweet as a summer butter
that lingers, as do your kisses, at length
upon my tongue, which draws your nectar out
from between elegant thighs, to quench thirst
uncured by lesser draught, the fiery gout
consuming us in the moment loins burst
and I am greedy for your tender taste,
I waste nothing, for it empowers me
as you perform the dance of chaos, laced
with fresh endorphins and the green fairy
of your romantic fantasies, reserve
only to our betters, withheld to serve.

VIII only to our betters, withheld to serve

only to our betters, withheld to serve
to lesser, ardent, suitors, omega
and beyond, the bondage we must deserve
to appreciate our time, as data
winds the clocks and we can only count down
the unknowable span that limits us
in exactly how many times we crown
and clown and frown before the treasonous
and intemperate make their shallow case
for our execution to bloodthirsty
and apathetic juries of the bass
fools, collateral damage their mercy.
destiny masters, in the end, confess
the illusion of our unworthiness.

VIIII the illusion of our unworthiness

the illusion of our unworthiness,
for that is what it is, an illusion.
benefits no one, not ourselves, and less
the liars and lost who propagate, done
with truth and the essence of it, faulty
dreams to make themselves taller by cutting
us down, that never works, melancholy
and madness feed sickly egos, gutting
sense and sanity in downward spiral
to the personal hells we habitate
while waiting for it all to be viral
and perfect the world that we love so much
but when I touch you or recall the touch…

X but when I touch you or recall the touch

but when I touch you or recall the touch
you gave to me on the stairway, invite
to the delight of your passions, held such
and then released, a feast of spirit's light
shining like a new sun upon me, raw
and savage and yet, somehow most sacred
like a pagan rite of passage to gnaw
away the crippling simplicity bred
of true failure to understand ardor
and the madness of your soul when we lose
control and give ourselves to the splendor
unfolding between us, open to choose
beautiful dreams, ignited by caress
you shared with me, taking that which we bless.

XI you shared with me, taking that which we bless

you shared with me, taking that which we bless
and make sacred in our hearts, the true faith,
that which is in ourselves, I must confess
I myself have stumbled more than once, wraith
of past madness has breached the veil and cursed
me with memory, that I care to beg
an end to my moral conscience, the thirst
for an end to torment is total, keg
of black powder under Parliament, sent
as a warning to those who have twisted
individual thought and discernment,
when all I ever wanted consisted
of being worthy of lover's true touch,
confessing hunger for each other such.

XII confessing hunger for each other such

confessing hunger for each other such
that we are humbled by the desire born
of the mere awareness, so very much,
of magic, music, and mystery torn
from ancient mythologies and made real,
as real as anything I have ever
borne witness to, true religion, ideal,
passionate in the extreme, I never
expected to be set upon by such
a rapture, rising up to crowd the clouds
and find evidence of all I could touch
previously only with my mind's shrouds.
we have slept for far too long in this night,
we are awakened to light and delight.

XIII we are awakened to light and delight

we are awakened to light and delight
to weave our prayers and spells in limbs and lips.
the sorceries in all degrees seize right
and wrong and make them relative as slips
of the tongue are most appreciated.
I trace the air and flowers bloom to fall,
petals askew, across your form, naked
and warm, radiating your silent call
for further wonders between us, witchcraft
and the devils that laughed when we fumbled
as we tumbled across nondescript graft
of bartered acts and promises, humbled
to be here with you in the fading light
as we make memories in sultry night.

XIIII as we make memories in sultry night

as we make memories in sultry night.
many memories. and then yet, some more
to bank for future reference and right
preferences. memory has a score
to settle with instinct, finding common
ground to grind what we can find, together
and to our liberation, temptation
and temperance, in the altogether,
feeling the friction of our most sacred
parts, lubricated by our oils, the spoils
of a war amicably ended, red
and solferino, intended swift foils
and fancy footwork, bitter days erased
accepting not what was offered, in taste,

XV accepting not what was offered, in taste (diadem)

accepting not what was offered, in taste,
of all the pleasant possibilities,
when we know there is fresh ambrosia, chaste
to the corruption of the low degrees
where we are malnourished and neglected
from a false sense that we do not deserve
to taste the nectar of Olympus, fed
only to our betters, withheld to serve
the illusion of our unworthiness,
but when I touch you or recall the touch
you shared with me, taking that which we bless,
confessing hunger for each other such
we are awakened to light and delight
as we make memories in sultry night.

Woebegone

I I feel and face your absence profoundly,

I feel and face your absence profoundly,
the silence, and warmth, and pressure missing,
as well as all those sweet magicks, soundly
that can segue from passionate kissing
to torrid lovemaking of a nature
of true lovers, cast together, inspired
by the beauty of their coupling, the pure
essence of life consummated, required
by one another's needs and desires, soft
and urgent, all senses engaged, focused
on our paramours, poetry aloft,
rising to a certain purpose, locust
in the desert, all sustenance destroyed,
there is a vacant spot next to me, void.

II there is a vacant spot next to me, void

there is a vacant spot next to me, void
of heat but not of memory, I know
what you have done and would do, I avoid
surrendering to your exit, the slow
and wasteful emotion seeking to lay
upon me, smother my rhapsody to
a sleep of death of my heart, but I stay
alive and vigilant for you, anew
whispering your urgencies, soft tremors
building to a rattle, tattling on our
night's festival of memory, embers
flaming as the walls crack and split, power
at the precipice, we speak profoundly
of the needed heat of your heart, soundly.

III of the needed heat of your heart, soundly

of the needed heat of your heart, soundly
it is known to me, if no other, held
even in the deepest doubts and roundly
denounced out of necessity, you've shelled
this guarded soul and made a meal of it,
more than once, but it is an immortal
essence that, even in despair, can sit
calmly in the fires, await the portal
that shall bring me to you or you to me
so that, whatever the circumstances,
we can be together and face banshee
keens determined to end summer dances
ere they have begun, but we merge, alloyed,
set on never sleeping apart, avoid!

IIII set on never sleeping apart, avoid

set on never sleeping apart, avoid
the void we are inevitable to,
reaching out with prayerful hands, paranoid,
the end of all things that are new and true,
whispers shake the ceiling and the faintest
draft becomes the hurricane, fierce and raw,
to tear life from me, to deny my best
intentions and inventions, the heart's law
overturned and joy denied, injustice
in the face of expectations, thrown down
with a savage roar that encompasses
and shatters my glass soul and mocking crown
that signified hope, now in vanity
but something more profound, profanity.

V but something more profound, profanity

but something more profound, profanity
to the forgotten gods of childhood torn,
torn from us in rapacious villainy,
unable to accept Nazarite's shorn
locks and betrayal, blinded in the pain
of the wrenching of my heart from my chest,
the cleansing baptism gives way to stain
and the flow of polluted blood, the test
of endurance to be walking barefoot
of hot broken glass and brass caltrops, traps
and challenges for the tempered with soot
and the illusion of strength, Atlas caps
the sky so I cannot escape this fraud
and cruel subversion of the will of God.

VI and cruel subversion of the will of God

and cruel subversion of the will of God
tests the faith and persistence of lovers
dependent on at least slightly skewed odd
in their favor, but with table covers
pulled out from under the grail, we tumble
end over end and spend time in limbo,
waiting for the revelations' crumble
in the candid coherent light's morrow
hiding evidence from us if we choose
to be our victims of denial, sent
to the back of the class to give up, lose
the opportunity to make advent
in selfish anguish, our insanity
for we were woven, for this vanity.

VII for we were woven for this vanity

for we were woven for this vanity
for this self-absorption that seals our fate
in the revocation of sanity
in the name of fury turned inward, hate
and degradation, the public display
of bitterness and inability
to rise up, not just to fly, but to lay
foot to asphalt and, with civility
walk out the door into blasphemous night
that rends and rips and corrupts the fabric
of our mosaic memories, the light
no longer our companion, end tragic
unless we can rise and find us a God,
the reflection of our best virtues, laud.

VIII the reflection of our best virtues, laud

the reflection of our best virtues, laud
the lover, even when unrequited,
requiem for our worst, lifeless façade
more ash than fire, true desire despited
for our failing sight, lack of vision guides
us into the roughest of paths, as does
a questing heart, true heroes fail the tides
but seek the path of honor, nonetheless.
redefining love and lover in doubt
that what we knew was myths and mysteries
filling in the ignorant holes without
substance or any more truth, histories.
but there is fire on the horizon, fresh
the design and the intention to mesh.

VIIII the design and the intention to mesh

the design and the intention to mesh
flesh to flesh is not always destiny.
sometimes we must make our own fates, the fresh
zest of awakenings, striving, many
knocks on the door are ignored, our entry
delayed if allowed at all as our suit
is considered, sly calculations be
working in the ether, our best refute
of free will is the perplexing concept
that we choose who to love, in obsessing
in a way that lays us prone to incept
the soft brilliance of the carnal blessing
once obscure, but now obvious, once blind
in all manner of things, even to find.

X in all manner of things, even to find

in all manner of things, even to find
as chaotic as clothes strewn in a path
to the bedroom, if we are so inclined
to take the options presented, the bath
of purification, our sweat as smooth
baptism, connecting to the most holy
creations of the Creator, a truth
often overlooked, even the lowly
are too proud to admit that they are held
in the spell and spiral of emotions
when the thunderbolt strikes and we are spelled
by the rain of fluids that fill oceans
while we seek to find and bind in the flesh
our places in the pattern we refresh.

XI our places in the pattern we refresh

our places in the pattern we refresh
with our presence as we pass through this world
to pick our paths with all of thought and flesh
to reach an unimaginable burled
colossus, grown in pine and oak and yew,
it wasn't until unexpectedly
you had mounted me I finally knew
you wanted me, just as you counted me
easy to capture, but to hold, a test
of tantalus affection, intellect,
and a sense of the complexity best
understood after a long coit, respect
on one who has found the new sky, aligned
the horizon then look until made blind.

XII the horizon! then look until made blind

the horizon! then look until made blind.
see the shadows of things yet to come to
the present in this place, we will yet find
that nothing is impossible, if you
cast aside the notion that what we are
is what we were before we found our hearts
in synchronized patterns that transcend far
more than the limits of the meeting parts
that shift our minds to overdrive and peel
out, the limits of imagination
struck, then deconstructed as we reveal
what we had hidden away for ration
of the improbable, as we near it
by the radiance of rebirth, spirit!

XIII by the radiance of rebirth, spirit

by the radiance of rebirth, spirit
becomes something greater, we find purpose
in purgatory, the story of fit
feast released for the consummation plus
all the inestimable side dishes,
the infinite color wheel, now serving
more than the basketed loaves and fishes
but the full dimensions undeserving
we are of the legacy of stardust,
but it falls to us, inheritors found
in ramshackle finery, peace and lust
both captured by the winds in the resound
of our curses, verses in an obit.
transcendent in our bliss, as we near it.

XIIII transcendent in our bliss, as we near it

transcendent in our bliss, as we near it.
we find it in memories and actions
to experience what we inherit
from ancient lovers who risked transactions
of limitless value for a pocket
filled with lint and candy wrappers, plastic
to be thrown away with used condoms, wet
with shared experience but not drastic
and flurried, hurried rising, luxuria
without vision or affection to bear
the pressure mounting, counting fury a
sign of desire, of fire, of lover's prayer
for redemption. as with sharp fear soundly
I feel and face your absence profoundly,

XV I feel and face your absence profoundly (diadem)

I feel and face your absence profoundly,
there is a vacant spot next to me, void
of the needed heat of your heart, soundly
set on never sleeping apart, avoid!
but something more profound, profanity
and cruel subversion of the will of God,
for we were woven for this vanity,
the reflection of our best virtues, laud
the design and the intention to mesh
in all manner of things, even to find
our places in the pattern we refresh
the horizon then look until made blind
by the radiance of rebirth, spirit
transcendent in our bliss, as we near it.

Whereupon

I so many truths, many consequences

so many truths, many consequences,
from the slightest of fibs to the great lies
we tell, oft from desperation senses
of necessity to flee before skies
rain down the tears and beatings that you fear
if you do not have sanctuary to
retreat to when you are overwhelmed, hear
to death (or at least the perception), you
do what you must and I, the gullible
romantic, open my doors and welcome
you to my corner of the world, trouble
though there may be following when the sum
of the equation is to give hard pause,
that sometimes we don't connect to the cause.

II that sometimes we don't connect to the cause

that sometimes we don't connect to the cause
the effect, we reject what we do not
want to hear, clear signs of deception, flaws
in amber from which we clamber when caught,
often too late if we want to hold on
to all of our limbs, for we stepped, inept
on the ground we were promised, liaison,
a professed innocent angel, who leapt
into our arms with charms that would damn saints
and make a mockery of monks trading
gods for goddesses, the temple's constraints
notwithstanding, empathy engaging
too easily. in deception and need
the balance is not guaranteed, we feed.

III the balance is not guaranteed, we feed

the balance is not guaranteed, we feed
on often whatever is offered first,
or with the best presentation, our need
or desires set aside to bring us, cursed
and cursing out of our comfort zones, stones
for bread, tears for rain, and epic refrain
that warned us, red flags in bags, barren bones
instead of an oasis from the pain
and loneliness, hunkered in our bunker
from apocalyptic ambience, scars
weeping still while we are lead spelunker
on Orpheus' incursion, memoirs
in mysteries poetic, cunning clause
on our own definitions, our own laws.

IIII on our own definitions, our own laws

on our own definitions, our own laws
are tribal and obscure as we are sure
that we understand referenced, in cause
and ineffectual language, to cure
our contracts with ourselves, the paperwork
that gets shuffled and lost in time, in time,
for few things are forever, our kneejerk
reactions to the fractions of life, prime
to partial impartiality felt
but never confessed, we wrest holy grails
from the apostles to claim ourselves dealt
a winning hand in a losing game, sails
set for an unseen horizon, prison
and flaws. I have fallen and have risen.

V and flaws. I have fallen and have risen

and flaws. I have fallen and have risen,
but I have my flaws, cracked aspects that will
never fully heal, if they'd ever been
complete and intact, for every skill
there are two vulnerabilities, cold
eyes find them easily enough and there
is where they hit, to split the seed I hold
within me, striving for the better air
to catch my wings of wax and feathers, lift
and gift me with perspective and a view
of what the world really looks like adrift
in the sky, from on high, fortunate few
are allowed to climb high so dreams commence,
always hoping to make the better sense.

VI always hoping to make the better sense

always hoping to make the better sense
of the senselessness of the human heart
I lay down my oracular suspense
and spyglass to face what is truly part
of my corner of reality. I
have to admit, it is you. I may not
understand everything you lay high
upon your card table, but I allot
and allow that, here and now, you make me
want to be a better person that I
might feel less unworthy, even more free
to spend time I have left to multiply
our blessings and break from the bleak crimson
of the way the universe works, prison.

VII of the way the universe works, prison

of the way the universe works, prison
seems an apt metaphor, the bars may be
not always visible and tactile, none
of the obvious trappings, but you see…
anyplace with boundaries that contain
us is a prison, if we allow it
to swallow our hope and peace, to make pain,
even in the philosophical fit
of seeking freedom in four dimensions,
walking free of the bounds and wards of time,
reliving in memory affections
offered and accepted in the harsh climb
towards our finding purpose and sentience
to our entire life and experience.

VIII to our entire life and experience

to our entire life and experience,
we answer to only ourselves unless
we choose to submit to the greater sense
of releasing our boundaries, confess
that we have discovered something better,
brighter, and more divine than our mirror,
which is silver and glass, ego's fetter
that drags us down and holds us back, clearer
than we dare admit, it is light shadows
pantomiming a shallow fraud, loveless
and uncertain in the spirit's necrose
as poets in us wax lustrous, luckless,
bloodied fists for light and love forgotten,
I have been so lonely and crestfallen.

VIIII I have been so lonely and crestfallen

I have been so lonely and crestfallen,
being left by the road side, random toad
grazed by a Mitsubishi, drunk driven
when you're still on probation for the load
of shit you handed out when you side swiped
a row of student parking, hurrying
to trade a piece of ass for some pills, striped,
pretty colors, second hand 'script boring
a hole in your stomach, but a fair trade
in your perceptions, staggering and glazed,
another lost junkie in the parade,
who found beauty is currency, amazed
by rate of exchange in my darkest night.
but I have also known joy and delight.

X but I have also known joy and delight

but I have also known joy and delight,
passionate embraces and faces not
to be lost in the kaleidoscope's light
that floods my mind when I allow it, taught
to never give up, even when slaughtered
by impossible odds, my inner eye
always willing to risk, but not watered
by too many tears to see the truth, pry
my nictating membrane open and find
the greatest weapon in my arsenal,
my great folly and the power to bind
myself to my deities, to not fall
by any hand but my own, and all in
a child's sense of glee at pear tree pollen.

XI a child's sense of glee at pear tree pollen

a child's sense of glee at pear tree pollen,
falling like a Hindu blessing, colors
crisp and complete, so sweet you can call in
for a mental Margarita, cover
your ass and catch a jet to Venice, blame
me if you are found out, I've little doubt
but that there's a bus you can hide your shame
by throwing me under, the most devout
need outs for explaining to a husband
who is not quite as divorced as you'd said
until after the night in my bed, stand
and face the scrutiny, he wants me dead
but it was an experience, that one night
gold and purple and red, the colors bright.

XII gold and purple and red, the colors bright

gold and purple and red, the colors bright,
the tastes and textures perplexing, the sound
of your voice, a whisper or a cry, right
and intimate, infinite as the ground
falls away and we play at being born
yet one more time, forgetting all before
to soar on borrowed wings to the sworn
that leave us satiated, craving for
just another ocean to cure our thirsts,
the giants' test of our true intentions
and persistence, resistance fills and bursts
the barriers of flesh and our mentions
of God cast us to a recovery,
glary, the wonder of discovery.

XIII glary, the wonder of discovery

glary, the wonder of discovery,
I would say I love you, but you hate that,
so ancient and simplistic, calvary
in a theology of the were-cat
mewling and yet fooling no one but me
because I want to be swept up, away
in a fine romance, naïve and I see
only the adornments, not the grim grey
under the potions and lotions you wear
to feel liberated from who you are,
who is pretty incredible, but where
you are misled is believing each scar
is shame, it is the magic of faerie
that refreshes us to recovery.

XIIII that refreshes us to recovery

that refreshes us to recovery.
that lets us rise as a part of us dies
and decomposes in the cosmos, free
we are made to remake the worlds and skies
in a palette and geometry to
suit us better than these old clothes, worn, torn,
ultimately boring and a renew
for the old visions fading and reborn
to our fresh sparking of the quintessence
to create fires unimagined by those
content to wear ridiculous old clothes
when they look better wet and naked, rose
petals and honeysuckle defenses.
so many truths, many consequences.

XV so many truths, many consequences (diadem)

so many truths, many consequences
that sometimes we don't connect to the cause.
the balance is not guaranteed, we feed
on our own definitions, our own laws
and flaws. I have fallen and have risen,
always hoping to make the better sense
of the way the universe works, prison
to our entire life and experience.
I have been so lonely and crestfallen,
but I have also known joy and delight,
a child's sense of glee at pear tree pollen,
gold and purple and red, the colors bright,
glary, the wonder of discovery
that refreshes us to recovery.

Denouement

I no, there are no endings except in tales

no, there are no endings except in tales.
all is infinite, no one short story
fills the never-ending scrolls where the nails
leave bloody rivulets, sign of glory
of a great battle, or a martyr, or
a passionate embrace face to face in
perfect eschatology in prayer for
yet another extraordinary spin
as a fevered dervish, overcome by
the energies entering and fleeing
our bodies in a perfect cycle, high
tantrism and the bending of our being.
the universe recalls our coit and court,
told when memory fails or time is short.

II told when memory fails or time is short

told when memory fails or time is short,
the unpronounceable glyphs that show us
what was that we might build upon purport
instead of our own perceptions, discuss
to tertiary interpretations
but then it is not what was said or read
but the spoils of a conquest of nations
with no purpose whatsoever, we've bled
enough that the folly of contention
is obvious. I want you because you
give me a sense of joy and creation,
that there is God and our hearts must breakthrough
before our starship, when the sunlight fails
and we want to put the kids to sleep, sails.

III and we want to put the kids to sleep, sails

and we want to put the kids to sleep, sails
unfurled to safely navigate dreamlands
that otherwise may contain wicked gales
to cast them from their course, upon the strands
of shattered glass sands that will cut their feet
and hobble them into tragic nightmares
when we wish them the best of dreams, the sweet
innocence they can hold onto as heirs
to a world we seek to make a better
place, to build the sense of wonder we want
to always hold onto, beyond letter
and law, we wish to bid them well, not daunt
their exuberance as they grow, consort
set for their dreamland, childhood's soft passport

IIII set for their dreamland, childhood's soft passport

set for their dreamland, childhood's soft passport
lets them explore and imagine what their
world will be, what they may see, in transport
far from bedroom walls and darkened halls where
barriers, virtual but effective
give us our rest and solace, the moments
where eternal optimism will give
us the strength to re-enact the movements
between everyday and everynight, soft
kisses and the passionate hisses sighed
in hungers undenied, lovers' slide oft
repeated to build the tempest fest, pried
from our sustained lives pride and vexities
to distant lands welcomed complexities.

V to distant lands welcomed complexities

to distant lands welcomed complexities
to add a rich lifescape to our own, dreams
pile on infinite stacks of our own ease,
melting and running like the morning streams
of consciousness untangling from the night,
where we are in control of tapestries
that stretch, horizon to horizon, light
silks unfurling in the inconstant breeze,
bidding for our attentions, intentions,
without exaggeration, pretention,
but with ten thousand most holy mentions
in the scriptures of our lives, ascension
and revelation of souls, days to come
and vexities of grown life await them.

VI...and vexities of grown life await them

...and vexities of grown life await them
who are brave enough to step on the blades
of time weavers, believers kiss the hem
of the elected, dancers in parades
spinning flag and banner to flash colors
high and about, the drums sound and we find
that our love can be unkind if lovers
do not lay sacred seal on the vault signed
in blood and tears by the brightest sellers
of truth and evidences seen first hand
on the limitless plains of joy, tellers
of amomancies and the chasm spanned
by those brave enough to follow the breeze
over the horizon, behind the trees.

VII over the horizon, behind the trees

over the horizon, behind the trees,
we hide from all others, but not ourselves
for we have seen the quintessence at ease
by true lovers committed to themselves
to find a way to live and fight and play
with sophistication and innocence,
a kiss is still a kiss and shows the way
to the edge of the world if the pretense
is stripped away, and we stand unashamed
in the brisance of the dawn of tomorrow,
warm and wound about one another, claimed
and revealed in the fields of Arbol, no
more the eyes cast down in shadows of rhumb,
where mysteries wait discovery from.

VIII where mysteries wait discovery from

where mysteries wait discovery from
we will find most answers that we dare seek,
and more than a few unexpected, come
with me and let us explore coeur rage, speak
the word you swore to take to love and war
and I will be there with you, beside you
at all times, balancing unity for
the identity of self. the birds flew
in ancient skies and still remain to fill
the blue, and we will endure immortal
to the rendering of time and thought, will
and our faith that this is the first portal,
not the last, and we are cast and to last
one end of the rainbow to the other.

VIIII one end of the rainbow to the other

one end of the rainbow to the other.
colors and intensities to bathe in,
to make our sacred bed upon, smother
your apprehensions, enwrap and swathe in
satins and silks and sackcloth, all manner
of the fabric of reality, textures
of time and space and dimensions, Vanir
and Aesir, all of the gods lay fractures
of their realities at our feet, for
our dispensations, for they fade away
in a new day of love and hope and more
than a glimmer of peace, coming in stay
to offer chance for an end to sorrows
so now we pass through unknown tomorrows.

X so now we pass through unknown tomorrows

so now we pass through unknown tomorrows
with little more than one another for
comfort in the face of joys and sorrows
that come on their own schedule and pace, more
sometimes than we had prepared for, but we
are strong and draw more strength not just from one
another, entanglement creates three
of the twain, and we are greater than sun
and the stars, for we can reason and form
new magicks out of the nature of life,
a sprig of this, a petal of that, warm
between us and find something that no strife
can ever sever as now we gather
with the confidence of lovers, rather.

XI with the confidence of lovers rather

with the confidence of lovers rather
than the cowardice of the hesitant
who think the better of the dice, blather
about security, but negligent
in stepping up to the purpose of time,
to be marked off with evolution, not
entropy, waiting for the worms, a crime
in every sense, stealing and sealing hot
wax to hide the talents uninvested
to the displeasure of the investor,
timidity? not for lovers, tested,
found wanting, the cold taunting jester
mocks solitude, your sullen tomorrows
tempered with love and life, joys and sorrows

XII tempered with love and life, joys and sorrows

tempered with love and life, joys and sorrows,
our merged existence is to be revealed,
excited over, happiness borrows
to pay dividends in the long run, healed
are the scrapes, forgotten like a skinned knee
you received in childhood. far in the past
you have better things to do than to flee
into shadows at first sight of light cast
by a warming sun to help you grow strong
and see the world around you, no wonder
the first gods were the sun gods, we belong
to a species that respects the thunder
but we must lay close, against fear persist
shared in a synergy that can resist.

XIII shared in a synergy that can resist

shared in a synergy that can resist
anything fate can throw at it, passion
staggers sometimes under the iron fist
of all the shit the world summons, ashen
countenances requiring blood and more,
the taste of a lover's surrender, trust
enough to give over all restraint for
the curious fury of desire, lust
and crusty rust over revelation
the necessity of intimacy,
all forms, giving pleasure, motivation
for further exchange of ultimacy
proving false critics and prophets who twist
the doubts and dreadnaughts of those who persist.

XIIII the doubts and dreadnaughts of those who persist

the doubts and dreadnaughts of those who persist.
vanguard and residual force, the course
is laid out before us and our hearts, kissed
from an unexpected quarter, is force
unto itself. pax vobiscum, I could
hold this kiss for a thousand lifetimes, but
the appetizer is not the feast, good
is unto itself, but greater? we shut
the doors and dim the lights for the tonights
heal us, reveal us to one another
that we are empowered to see the sights
hidden from mortal eyes, pledged to other
senses, past our defenses, setting sails.
no, there are no endings except in tales.

no, there are no endings except in tales
told when memory fails or time is short
and we want to put the kids to sleep, sails
set for their dreamland, childhood's soft passport
to distant lands welcomed complexities
and vexities of grown life await them
over the horizon, behind the trees
where mysteries wait discovery from
one end of the rainbow to the other.
so now we pass through unknown tomorrows
with the confidence of lovers rather
tempered with love and life, joys and sorrows
shared in a synergy that can resist
the doubts and dreadnaughts of those who persist.

About the Author

William F. DeVault has, in his creative run (so far) amassed tens of thousands of poems (and those are just the ones that passed his first reading). He has authored 25+ books, received his unfair share of sobriquets, and performed his poetry all over the continental United States and throughout cyberspace. He has read in churches, bars, parks, schools, libraries, and brothels.

Married twice, divorced twice, but still the romantic optimist, he has fathered three children in whom he is well pleased, and mentored dozens of poets. He founded and facilitated the **Romantic and Erotic Poetry Group** for America Online, and that service's **Passionate Craft** poetry workshop, and been facilitator for **Authors in Conversation** for the **Bronx Book Fair**, this fall he is being honored on National Beat Poetry Day in Ocen City, Maryland.

He was named the **Romantic Poet of the Internet** by Yahoo in 1996 and the **US National Beat Poet Laureate** by the National Beat Poetry Foundation for 2017-2018. Some consider him the **Poet Laureate of the Internet** for his presence and pioneering use of the internet during and even before the mid-1990's. He is a founding member in the **Rolling Stock Poets** reading group.

Lightning Source UK Ltd.
Milton Keynes UK
UKHW051907301222
414659UK00008B/240